THE INTELLIGENT MICRO
Artificial intelligence for microcomputer

Brighton College of Technology
LIBRARY

Richmond Terrace
Brighton, East Sussex, BN2 2SZ.
Brighton 685971 Ext. 284.

This book is to be returned on or before the last date stamped above

104741

The Intelligent Micro
Artificial intelligence for microcomputers

Noel Williams

McGRAW-HILL Book Company (UK) Limited

London · New York · St Louis · San Francisco · Auckland · Bogotá
Guatemala · Hamburg · Johannesburg · Lisbon · Madrid · Mexico
Montreal · New Delhi · Panama · Paris · San Juan · São Paulo · Singapore
Sydney · Tokyo · Toronto

Published by
McGRAW-HILL Book Company (UK) Limited
MAIDENHEAD · BERKSHIRE · ENGLAND

British Library Cataloguing in Publication Data

Williams, Noel
 The intelligent micro: artificial intelligence
 for microcomputers.
 1. Artificial intelligence—Data processing
 2. Sinclair QL (Computer)
 I. Title
 001.53′5′0285404   Q336

 ISBN 0–07–084770–3

Library of Congress Cataloging in Publication Data

Williams, Noel.
 The intelligent micro.
 Includes index.
 1. Artificial intelligence—Data processing.
 2. Microcomputers. 3. Sinclair QL (Computer)—
 Programming. 4. Basic (Computer program language)
 Q336.W55 1985   001.64   85–12486
 ISBN 0–07–084770–3

Copyright © 1986 McGraw-Hill Book Company (UK) Limited. All rights reserved. No part of this publication may be reproduced, stored in a retrieval system, or transmitted, in any form or by any means, electronic, mechanical, photocopying, recording, or otherwise, without the prior permission of McGraw-Hill Book Company (UK) Limited, or of the original copyright holder.

12345 LT 88765

Printed and bound in Great Britain by Latimer Trend & Company Ltd, Plymouth, Devon

*For Steven and much more
than friendship*

Contents

Preface	xi
Chapter 1 What is artificial intelligence?	1
1.1 Introduction	1
1.2 Defining intelligence	2
Chapter 2 AI on micros	8
2.1 Aspects of AI	8
2.2 Robotics	8
2.3 Pattern recognition	9
2.4 Creativity	9
2.5 Problem solving and decision making	9
2.6 Learning	10
2.7 Natural language processing	10
2.8 Personality theory	11
2.9 Human–computer interaction	11
2.10 Program conversion notes	12
Chapter 3 Creativity	19
3.1 Creativity basics	19
3.2 Making a joke	22
3.3 Creating ideas	25
3.4 Improving the idea generator	35
Chapter 4 Artistic creativity	39
4.1 But is it art?	39
4.2 Sentence generator	41
4.3 Creating poetry	46
4.4 Versificator—the program	52
4.5 Creating a story	53

Chapter 5 Understanding natural language — 58
5.1 General considerations — 58
5.2 A two-word parse — 59
5.3 Getting words — 65
5.4 Augmented transition network grammars — 67
5.5 The ATN program — 74

Chapter 6 Pattern matching — 86
6.1 Introduction — 86
6.2 Spelling and style — 87
6.3 Speech acts — 89
6.4 Threat — 91
6.5 Speech — 96
6.6 Machine translation — 99

Chapter 7 Memory — 104
7.1 Human memory — 104
7.2 Synonym chains — 105
7.3 Semantic networks — 111
7.4 Frames — 112
7.5 Conceptual dependency — 114
7.6 Scripts — 120

Chapter 8 Meaning and learning — 124
8.1 The need to learn — 124
8.2 Making comparisons — 125
8.3 How does the program work? — 132
8.4 A destructive machine — 135
8.5 The syllogism program — 137

Chapter 9 Reasoning, inference and experts — 148
9.1 Inference — 148
9.2 Infer—the program — 150
9.3 Expert systems — 157
9.4 Heuristics — 160
9.5 Miniex — 166

Chapter 10 Personal computers with personalities — 170
10.1 Personality and intelligence — 170
10.2 Building a personality program — 172

10.3 A simple approach	175
10.4 Responsive programs	180
10.5 Decoding personality	181
10.6 Kelly grid—how it works	182

Chapter 11   Postscript—the intelligent micro   192

Bibliography   195

Index   196

Preface

If you want to learn about a fascinating new application of computers or to begin to learn the principles behind some new computing skills, then this book will do both things for you. It provides a wide and detailed introduction to artificial intelligence (AI) which involves many novel approaches to programming. It can also result in programs which are more satisfying to use and develop than your average game or database because the computer behaves, in some measure, like a human being.

The book is built around 13 programs which use artificial intelligence techniques, plus some additional routines and algorithms. The programs are written in Sinclair SuperBASIC, which is the language used on the QL. This is one of the most advanced BASICs around and is therefore eminently suitable for this kind of work. However, all the programs have been designed to be as easy to understand as possible, and conversion to other BASICs is elementary. In fact I recommend that owners of machines other than the QL carry out such conversion. Two things will be learned: (a) why a highly structured language like SuperBASIC is desirable for AI programming; and (b) that AI routines can be written for just about any machine you care to name. Conversion notes from QL to BBC, C64 and Spectrum are given in Chapter 2.

All programs are tested and working and can easily be adapted to your own purposes. The programs are mainly used to illustrate a wide range of topics which are becoming increasingly important in modern software design, rather than to give you fully operational robots or complex intelligent databases (either of which would require a book much longer than this one). Their main aim is therefore to introduce you to the fascinating and varied fields of work comprising artificial intelligence by showing the range of human capabilities that machines are beginning to possess. Particular attention is given to text processing and natural language because this is an area which everybody can understand. Language is crucial for making software friendly, so if you want educational programs that can chat to the student, databases that can be questioned using ordinary English, or adventure games with commands several sentences long, you will find plenty here to help you along.

But artificial intelligence is a new science and constantly breaking new ground. This means that you will find no easy solutions to real problems which require intelligent software, and in many cases programmers have only just begun to understand the nature of the problems they are exploring. The achievements of AI come nowhere near its potential or its aims. Although there is no such thing as an intelligent machine, this book can show you some of what is involved in creating one. A bibliography is provided so that you can pursue those areas of most interest at your leisure. You should always remember in AI research, however, that the field is so new that your ideas may well be original and it is perfectly possible that you, sitting at home with a micro, will develop AI ideas with capabilities and cleverness in an area not even contemplated by researchers at IBM or MIT.

As no system can yet claim true intelligence, and no book can show you how such a complete system might be achieved, my aim has been to give programs which begin to make micros human-like. Intelligence is a complex and multi-faceted phenomenon and it is only by individual exploration of each of the facets of human intelligence and behaviour that we can gradually advance towards a completely intelligent system which combines all such features (assuming such a thing is desirable). By the time you have finished the book you will be able to write programs that can correctly analyse sentences, write poetry, create jokes, make decisions on complex evidence, recognize threats and make inferences—programs that begin to think, to learn and to 'understand'. But, more important than this, you will also understand how such programs work and why they are limited, so that you can go on to develop better and more capable programs of your own.

It would be a mistake to pretend that a program can be fully intelligent. All we can do at present is simulate various aspects of human intelligence with some degree of accuracy. You will find that even in those areas where AI has had major success, such as with expert systems, researchers can be puzzled by their own successes. We are only just on the fringes of an exciting new form of computing and there are an enormous number of puzzles which need solving. You could be involved in the solution of some of them.

This book would still be lying on my desk were it not for the affection and hard work of Carrol, who deserves all the thanks she can get.

[Note: The listings in this book are taken directly from running programs. However, the printer used has shown each # sign as a £ sign. Therefore, wherever a £ sign is encountered it should be replaced with a # sign.]

1 What is artificial intelligence?

1.1 Introduction

As computers, microprocessors and microcomputers become more and more important in our lives we hear more and more about artificial intelligence, about intelligent knowledge-based systems (or expert systems), about the Japanese fifth generation of microcomputers and the Alvey report on Britain's need for an equivalent research project. What is all the fuss about? And why is it happening now?

One of the reasons for the rapid growth of interest in artificial intelligence (let us agree to call it AI for the rest of this book so that you do not get fed up with the persistent phrase), is the new set of microcomputers becoming available, such as the QL, Apricot and IBM PC, with faster and larger processors and much larger memories than the 64K available to the tired old 6502 and Z80 micros we are so familiar with. Because micros with 128K, 256K or even half a megabyte of RAM are now coming into the price range of anyone who can afford a second mortgage, interest is growing in applications which can use that massive extra RAM. Partly this is because people with large computers tend to feel that they are not using them properly (whatever that means) if they are not using all the extra memory, and partly because developments in AI have always been held back by the expense of suitable hardware. Now most micro enthusiasts have the potential to begin developing their own original investigations of the limits and rewards of AI programming. Just as an enormous series of developments has taken place in hardware and software in the wake of the video games boom, so it seems likely that a similar 'explosion' of interest will occur when people sit down to think 'what worthwhile things can I do with my micro?'

The main aim of this book is to introduce you to some of the concepts of AI but without being too theoretical and dull. On the one hand you will learn something about the general aims, achievements (and also the major problems) in AI programming; on the other hand you will find a number of illustrative programs that do somewhat clever things, most of which can easily be incorporated into larger programs or fitted together to construct more versatile routines. Although AI can be a difficult area of computer study, that does not mean that it has to be all the time, nor that it cannot be enjoyable. AI is above all things about people and that can make any subject interesting and entertaining. It also enables the micro enthusiast of today to enjoy some of the thrill of pioneering and discovery that fired the first home computer hobbyists five years ago, for AI is a very new kind of computing where new developments occur almost every day.

So the aims of this book are three:

1. to introduce you to a number of aspects of programming which are becoming increasingly important and which are collectively known as AI;
2. to show how BASIC can be used for writing AI routines, illustrated through one of the best BASICs available;
3. to illustrate some simple AI techniques and show how some of them can be adapted for use in your own programs. In particular we will pursue detailed investigation of various aspects of natural language and text processing because these are areas which can greatly enhance serious business programs, educational software and games like adventures and simulations.

One thing this book does not spend much time on is the kind of AI used in abstract games programs like chess and draughts. These routines consist largely of different search strategies. Search is an important concept, not only in AI but in other branches of programming, but the searches employed by most abstract games are often specific to the kind of game and as such are only of interest to writers of such games.

1.2 Defining intelligence

So what exactly is AI? There are many definitions, none of which are really comprehensive because just about anything that a computer does could be regarded as 'intelligent' in some sense. Does not something that can do quadratic equations, create moving graphics, measure the length of words and carry out the instructions of a human being seem intelligent to you? Well, you say, it depends what you mean by 'intelligent'. And that is the crux of the problem of definition. The nature of AI depends on what you think of as the nature of intelligence. Some people think that intelligence is no more than a complex series of rules for decisions and that if we knew enough about those rules and decisions we could write programs to carry them out, and the machines carrying out those programs would be exactly as intelligent as the human beings who originally held those rules and made those decisions. Others argue that 'intelligence' is something uniquely human, perhaps even God-given, and therefore it cannot be discovered, described or defined because it defines us. Then there are a number of people who are somewhere in between these two extremes who think that a lot of the activities we call intelligent behaviour actually are rule-governed activities, just like computer programs, but that maybe some intelligent activities are not like that and perhaps we will never know about some activities. You can even argue that it is the nature of intelligence that it cannot understand itself, so even if human intelligence is no more than a series of rules, human beings will not be able to discover them.

For example, it is reasonable to say that understanding the word 'RUN' requires intelligence. We would know that someone understands this word if they carry out the operation that the word represents. So Sebastian Coe is intelligent because if you say 'RUN' to him he will lope off in a cloud of dust. Similarly your micro will carry out a series of activities if you type 'RUN'. But only if it has a program in it. Sebastian Coe shows his intelligence (though the lazier among us might prefer to think of it as stupidity) by carrying out a series of complex motor activities which, among other things, stop him from falling over and make sure that he gets from point A to point B in as short a time as possible. He is showing that he has a certain 'program', i.e., he has learned to act in certain ways in response to certain instructions. A program in a micro can be seen as the current state of learning of that machine and we can measure its intelligence by the accuracy with which it carries out its instructions, the efficiency with which it achieves the intended goal of those instructions and the number of inadequacies it has or errors it makes on the way.

From this point of view anything which carries out instructions, or responds to a signal, has some kind of intelligence. We can think of a kind of hierarchy of intelligence with stones pretty close to the bottom, plants slightly higher, insects a little higher, mammals rather higher and human beings (you and me anyway) somewhere near the top. On this kind of scale most micros would be between plants and insects. Plants respond to stimuli in a very restricted and highly conditioned way. If the light comes predominantly from the west, all the plants grow to the west. Maybe the light source is a lava flow which will frazzle the plants when they grow big enough, but they are not responsive enough to 'know' that.

Insects, on the other hand, not only respond in rather mechanical ways to stimuli, but they can create stimuli (i.e., they can 'give instructions'), they can learn and they can develop complex patterns of behaviour which have meanings, such as the dances that bees use to indicate a source of pollen. Most micros that I have been introduced to are not as clever as these bees. Micros can be given instructions and can carry them out, but they cannot instruct themselves. They cannot communicate with each other about things of interest to themselves. They cannot make decisions about which actions are in their best interests or in the interests of microcomputerdom in general. And where they are beginning to do such things it is not because they have 'discovered' how to do it but because humans have made the discovery and turned it into language sufficiently simple for the micro to understand.

So intelligence probably does not simply involve responding to stimuli and executing learned 'programs'. It involves other things as well. Psychology is the science which attempts to discover what these other things are and AI is one branch of psychology. Computer scientists are involved, linguists are involved, engineers are involved, philosophers are involved, but the main thrust of AI research comes from psychologists, because psychologists want to discover how human minds work. One way to make this discovery is to make a model of the human mind, just as we might demonstrate how a steam engine works by making a model, and AI is really about making models of human intelligence.

In this case the question 'Is the machine intelligent?' is almost meaningless. If you build a working model of a steam engine which does not look like a steam engine, but works like a steam engine, can do everything that a steam engine does and is a perfect replica in every significant detail of a real steam engine is your model a steam engine or not? Who cares? To all intents and purposes it is exactly like a 'real' steam engine. It behaves like a 'real' steam engine. If in some deep philosophical sense it is not a 'real' steam engine because it is smaller, or because it is not being used like one, or because it was not designed to be one, that hardly matters. In the same way it does not matter if an 'intelligent' dog actually thinks in a way we could not possibly understand which is nothing like our own intelligence. If the dog recognizes his mistress's voice, if he sits when told, if he fetches the paper when it is delivered and pines when his mistress is away, then he has a degree of intelligence. He understands what is going on around him and acts accordingly. The question of whether his intelligence is like our intelligence is unimportant.

So the argument boils down to a debate about the definition of words. When we talk about an intelligent machine, what we mean is a machine which, as far as we can tell, and within a limited area, acts as a human being would act in the same situation and with the same information. To understand this, just remember the Turing test. Alan Turing, an eminent mathematician in the thirties and forties, devised a test to determine whether a machine should be called intelligent or not. A human subject is placed in a room with two identical teletype terminals. All communication with the outside world takes place through those two terminals. Communicating with one terminal sits another human being, while the other is controlled by a computer. The human in the room has to determine which teletype is controlled by the computer and which by the human being. If he or she cannot decide, then, in every way that matters, the machine is as intelligent as the human being; it has passed the Turing test.

No machine has ever passed the test. But some have made some people think that they were human beings in special circumstances. For example Joseph Weizenbaum developed a program called 'Eliza' which simulates the responses of what is called a 'non-directive' psychiatrist, i.e., one who just tries to encourage patients to talk without passing any comment on what is being said. When his secretary first tried it out, she requested that he leave the room because she was holding a private conversation. As far as she was concerned, and even though she knew she was 'talking' to a computer program, it was an intelligent process which was 'taking her seriously'.

If we heavily restrict the kind of communication that is permitted through the teletype in applying a Turing-like test; for example, by restricting the topic of conversation, many machines and programs can be regarded as intelligent in a limited sense. What this means is that AI exists in a restricted form. There are machines which are intelligent in highly restricted areas. Psychologists and others have discovered some of the rules of some kinds of intelligence. Machines can imitate certain aspects of human behaviour. But no machine has anything like the flexibility, versatility or range of the dullest human being. However, such machines may not stay in the realms of science fiction for long and you may even be involved in bringing them to life—if you want to.

So there are only really two ways of defining AI which make any sense. One is to list all the things which people have called intelligent activities and which research has shown machines can model, and the other is to list all those things which people regard as intelligent behaviour which we might want machines to model but which no one has yet successfully made them model. The reason the last list is difficult to compile is because no one yet has a satisfactory definition of human intelligence or a satisfactory list of all the things that a human being can do which we might regard as intelligent. If we look at it from the ordinary person's point of view for a minute we might say that an activity appears clever if the person, creature or machine carrying it out satisfies one or more of three criteria:

1. It is doing something which we would not expect it to be able to do.
2. It is doing something we could not do or would find difficult to do.
3. It is doing something apparently with a purpose, intended to achieve a particular goal.

Criterion (1) simply means that our understanding or idea of the machine or creature is inadequate. Dogs might appear clever because we have a very limited idea of what a dog can or should be able to do. Criterion (2) simply means that we are inadequate in some sense—we are slower or weaker or illogical or have incomplete knowledge and so have not the ability to carry out the action. If we had the ability or the knowledge we might not regard it as special activity at all. For example if you understand machine code you regard it as easy, whereas everyone who cannot separate their bits from their bytes thinks you are particularly intelligent. In other words these definitions of 'intelligence' are relative to the person who is using them. When you know the secret you no longer regard it as intelligence.

Thus it is argued that computers that beat chess masters appear intelligent only to those who do not know the chess strategies and the programmed logic involved. You might argue in a similar way that chess masters appear intelligent only because we do not know what it is they are doing when they thrash us poor mortals at the game. But if we did know we might not regard it as intelligence at all. It seems clear that some of the things that a grand master does are the same as the things a computer does when deciding which piece to move—both 'know' something about previous games, both examine a number of different moves and look at their consequences, both try to balance the advantages for themselves against the advantages for the opponent. It is also clear that some of the things they are doing are different—the computer (in principle) might evaluate every possible move resulting from a particular position, whereas the grand master might 'feel' that a particular move looks promising and make his move on the strength of this feeling.

Criterion (3), however, is a useful one. Intelligence involves purpose and the purpose must come from the intelligent creature itself. This is a stumbling block with machines because they cannot really have any intentions. However they can be given goals, they can be given purposes which are extensions of the purpose of the programmer, and to this extent they have intelligence. The whole idea of 'strategy' depends on having a goal—a good strategic decision is one that brings you nearer the goal and a bad one is one that takes you away from it. Thus psychologists and AI researchers are very interested in goal-directed activity, the nature of strategy and 'why people do the things that they do'. Of course a major area for exploring the nature of strategic thinking is in games, and this is one area which can benefit from AI research.

If we now try to list the areas which have been explored with some success as a way of trying to define AI, the following list would cover most things:

1. pattern recognition and perception
2. robotics
3. creativity
4. problem solving
5. decision making
6. learning
7. natural language understanding
8. personality theory
9. human-computer interaction and the man–machine interface.

This is quite an assortment of areas and there is not room to cover them all with the same degree of detail in one book. However, you would probably agree that a machine which could create new ideas, hold a normal conversation, recognize the person talking to it, solve a variety of complex problems and make decisions about possible solutions, and could learn from its mistakes was either intelligent or a very good model of human intelligence. Unfortunately (or perhaps fortunately) there is no such machine and not likely to be one for some time, if ever. Though large claims have been made for work in nearly all these areas, and there certainly have been some notable advances, when you actually examine the achievements of AI they are not very spectacular. But they are interesting and there are several useful and fascinating areas of development. In particular it seems that if we are to have 'user-friendly' machines which most people will be happy with in a wide variety of situations, they need some of the routines provided by such work. So you might want to learn about AI simply to improve the so-called human interface between your software and its user. And this might apply whether you are producing a word processor or a mind-taxing adventure.

2 AI on micros

2.1 Aspects of AI

For the rest of this book we will forget the debate about the nature of machine intelligence and just assume that AI means 'making computers clever'. Whether you think they are actually clever or only models of cleverness is up to you. Let us also assume that you want to know about AI in order to write programs which are (or have some of the characteristics of) real human beings. We shall explore as many aspects of this as possible, as much to discover what the limitations of AI are as what can be done, and to see what needs to be understood in order to go past those limits. The rest of this chapter gives a brief description of each of the aspects of AI just listed, then examines some of the programming concepts involved and how they can be implemented in Sinclair SuperBASIC, and gives some notes on conversion to other BASICs. Then Chapter 3 begins the real analysis of AI, with chapters dealing with the topics described in this chapter—creativity, data storage and coding, natural language understanding and production, personality theory, pattern recognition, semantics, heuristics, learning, decision making and expert systems.

2.2 Robotics

Though robotics involves important work in AI it is not covered by this book as it is really about microcomputer control and sensors. The study of robotics is wide ranging, but broadly speaking the intelligence of robots can be described as very limited. Either a robot can only do exactly what it has been programmed to do, with no deviation or variation, such as the robot workers on assembly lines which exactly mimic human actions they have been programmed to copy, or, where they do have some degree of control over their environment, they are not able to carry out very important or sophisticated actions. In other words, the more useful the robot, the less intelligent it tends to be in practical terms. Understanding robots involves a great deal of knowledge of control systems and much less of AI.

2.3 Pattern recognition

However, in order to carry out any kind of action a robot has to know what it is acting on, and in this respect some robots have quite complex sensory apparatus for recognizing patterns. Some merely carry out actions blindly (literally), that they have been instructed to carry out and will spray the object in front of them in exactly the same way whether it is a car, a QL or a human being. But others can follow infra-red signals, or search for light sources, or recognize quite complex shapes when deciding whether an object is to be manipulated or not. AI has played a large part in describing what human beings pay attention to when they perceive things and in enabling machines to carry out similar operations.

In particular it is important for an intelligent system, whether it carries out control activities or simply provides a friendly interface for a database, to be able to recognize patterns of action in the world around it. The activities we call 'perception' do not simply involve the passive reception of signals, but active interpretation—even at the most fundamental level. The brain is constantly on the look-out for patterns of all kinds (including 'patterns of patterns') and it is this facility which allows it to sort out ambiguous messages and process information efficiently, whether its owner is listening to music in a crowded hall, trying to shoot down a space invader or translating a text from Welsh to Urdu.

2.4 Creativity

Creativity is possessed by all human beings in greater or lesser degree. For example we all have the capacity to produce an infinite number of different original sentences, assuming we would want to do so. We can create new ideas, new objects and new words. For many people artistic creativity in particular is something that machines will never be able to capture. However, as we will see, there are some aspects of creativity at least that can be programmed, and it seems likely that several kinds of relatively structured types of creativity will eventually be available to micros. As in some measure all creative activities seem to involve similar processes, if the basics can be programmed then the QL can begin to write, compose, paint or sculpt—or at the very least to become a useful tool providing ideas for a human being who wants to do such things.

2.5 Problem solving and decision making

These 'thought processes' have been most successfully implemented in so-called expert systems, which we will examine later on. The ability to recognize or define a problem, to examine it until one or several solutions are found, to make a decision concerning the best possible solution and to act upon it seems to be a fundamental feature of intelligence. However, it is notable that human beings are rather better at creating problems than solving them. In this respect machines are no different. Nevertheless, where we have some understanding of the kinds of problems that are involved and the strategies for finding a solution, there have been some successes for research.

2.6 Learning

Learning is related to all the above activities, but particularly problem solving. It is little use being able to solve a problem if, the next time a similar problem comes along, we have to start from scratch to solve that one as well. It is much more efficient if the previous solution is remembered—or even better if the strategy which produced that solution is remembered (because problem-solving strategies are more general than individual solutions). To this end an intelligent being must learn which are the best approaches to particular kinds of problems. Learning machines of one kind or another do exist but, as with most aspects of AI, they can only learn within very strict parameters. There is a sense therefore in which they can only learn what the programmer has given them a capacity to learn, which means presumably that they can only learn what the programmer already knows and could have programmed in to start with. We will take a brief excursion into learning theory below.

2.7 Natural language processing

Language is one of those features which, it is said, separates humans from all other animals. We can communicate in a system of signs which bear no relation to the things they stand for. Computers, of course, have languages of sorts. However, computer languages are what are known as 'formal languages'. That is they are completely and thoroughly defined by a series of very strict rules and those rules cannot be altered or broken. If you break a rule of BASIC the best you can hope for is 'Syntax Error'.

Natural languages are not like formal languages. They do have rules, usually hundreds of them, but the rules are sometimes unclear and ambiguous, they can be changed, they vary from speaker to speaker and situation to situation, and no natural language can ever be fully written down because it is always changing. We will spend quite a long time looking at how to get the micro to 'understand' ordinary language and also how we might go about getting it to talk to us in a manner more friendly than we are used to, in particular because this seems a prime requisite for completely satisfactory human–computer interaction.

2.8 Personality theory

Personality is not strictly an aspect of intelligence, but if machines are to become more like human beings they must acquire some of the characteristics of human beings. It is interesting that several of the successes of AI have involved modelling particular types of human being, such as the paranoid and the Rogerian psychiatrist. It may be the case that it is rather easier to model types of human intelligence than 'pure' intelligence because different types of personality may actually process and use information in significantly different ways. Even if this is not the case, if a micro is to have goal-directed behaviour then it must have its own particular goals, and this means it has its own preferences, its own desires and consequently its own character. It seems to be true to say that advances can only be made in getting machines to understand (and particularly to understand language) if we program with a particular kind of human processor in mind.

But it is also important to have machines that understand the personalities of users if they are to act as doctors, consultants and educators (even, as some people speculate, 'friends'). A machine which is sensitive to the differing personalities of all its users, and the differing moods of each individual user, may well be more versatile and useful than many insensitive human beings.

2.9 Human–computer interaction

Human–computer interaction, while not really part of AI, is a closely related area. It is concerned with all the methods of improving the ways that humans and computers communicate with one another. So it is particularly involved in anything which makes using a computer more attractive or more natural for a human being, especially if that involves making the machine behave more like a human being. There is some evidence to suggest, however, that in certain situations people prefer machines which actually behave like machines rather than like people (for example some people prefer to consult machines about intimate problems because a machine does not understand and cannot cause embarrassment). In such situations the study of human–computer interaction is actually at odds with AI, but usually they work together—improving the intelligence in a machine generally improves its friendliness for a user.

2.10 Program conversion notes

SuperBASIC has been used throughout this book because it and the QL are in many ways the best choice for implementing AI on a home computer. The QL has a large RAM with potential for further expansion, has mass storage devices (though these are not as good as conventional disk drives) and can be used for parallel processing (but not from BASIC). SuperBASIC is highly structured, allows long variable names for self-documenting programs and implements recursion, all of which are desirable features for an AI language.

However, the programs in this book can easily be converted to other BASICs. The following notes should help you in the task of conversion. They cover the main differences between SuperBASIC and other popular BASICS: Commodore BASIC, as implemented on the C64, which is also quite similar to Microsoft BASIC; Spectrum BASIC; and BBC BASIC (the nearest equivalent to QL BASIC). Owners of C64s, Spectrums, BBCs, Electrons and MSX computers as well as QLs should therefore be able to use all the programs in this book.

Screen display
None of the programs use graphics or SuperBASIC's window facilities, but some print text in particular colours or on particular portions of the screen. This is done only to improve the appearance of the output and is not necessary to the logic of any of the programs.

So the best way to adapt screen display for your micro is to ignore any screen-handling commands and colour commands which are not implemented on your micro. Then, when you have the program up and running you can add niceties of display which use the special features of your micro. The colour commands to ignore are: INK, which sets the text foreground colour, PAPER and STRIP which effectively set text background colour.

The Spectrum can use some of these commands exactly as for the QL, but the Spectrum screen display is smaller so positioning will have to altered. C64 colours are controlled by POKEing values to screen memory, so each INK statement can be regarded as a screen POKE and each paper statement as a POKE plus inverse video. BBC owners have a host of approaches to colour to choose from. The nearest to the QL/Spectrum approach is to use Teletext graphics, but in modes other than 7 (e.g., if you are using an Electron) VDU

19 can be used to select the colours you require and VDU 17 to change them as necessary.

SuperBASIC's AT command prints text at a particular position on screen. All the programs use a screen of 40 columns by 25 lines, which can be matched on the BBC but not on the Spectrum and C64, so you will have to experiment until satisfactory displays are found.

Variable names

SuperBASIC permits long variable names which make a program self-documenting and easy to understand. These have been used throughout the book. In most programs no harm will result from replacing all variable names with a name formed from the first two characters of the long name. However, to guard against errors it is best to go through the program listing all the variables and putting the renamed version next to it before converting any of the code. You can then simply substitute the new name for the old one as you type the listing in, knowing there is no incompatibility of names. The Spectrum will force you to adopt a strategy like this. The BBC can use most of the names used by SuperBASIC without conversion. The C64 can, however, cause problems as some variable names can be long but only the first two letters count, so if you use long names and the program seems to fail check that there are no variable names with the same two initial characters.

Procedures

A feature of structured languages is the procedure. This is essentially a block of code which acts like a subroutine in other languages. Each procedure begins with a DEF PROC statement and ends with an END DEF statement. In BBC BASIC, procedures differ only in ending with ENDPROC. When a procedure is called in SuperBASIC it is simply a case of using its name. In BBC BASIC the call must be prefaced by 'PROC'.

Spectrum and C64 owners will have to convert procedures into subroutines. In order to make the conversion process as simple as possible it is best to carry out the following stages. Firstly go through the SuperBASIC program and write a list of all the procedure names and the lines at which they start. Then type into your micro a skeleton program consisting of REM statements and RETURN statements. Each REM statement serves as the equivalent of the defining statement of the procedure so it should contain the name of the procedure/subroutine, and each RETURN statement marks the positions of an END DEF statement. So, for example, the following SuperBASIC program excerpt:

14 THE INTELLIGENT MICRO

    200 DEF PROCtest
    210 PRINT "in test"
    220 END DEF test
    300 DEF PROCanother
    310 PRINT "in another"
    320 END DEF another

becomes

    200 REM test
    210 print "in test"
    220 RETURN
    300 REM another
    310 PRINT "in another"
    320 RETURN

Then in the main program each time SuperBASIC uses the procedure name replace this with a GOSUB to the appropriate line number.

One of the differences between procedures and subroutines is that the former enable the passing of parameters and the use of local variables. Local variables have been used in only one program and we will consider that below as a special case. Parameter passing occurs quite frequently, however. If a SuperBASIC procedure is defined with brackets after its name, then the letters in the brackets define variables which will be used by the procedure and which expect values to be passed to them when the procedure is called.

When this is the case C64 and Spectrum owners should explicitly assign values to variables of the same name before the subroutine call. For example, in the listing in Fig. 41 procedure 'word' is defined at line 540 with two parameters called 'type' and 'number'. If you look at lines 380 and 420 (for example) in the listing you will see calls to the procedure where different variable names follow the call. If we miss the other lines from the program it looks like this:

    380 word determiner, de__no
    420 word adjective, adj__no
    540 DEF PROCedure word (type,number)

At line 380 procedure word is called, the value of variable determiner is passed to the parameter type and the value of variable de__no is passed to the parameter number. At line 420 procedure word is called again, but this time it is the value of variable adjective which is passed to parameter type and the value of variable adj__no which is passed to number. In Commodore BASIC (which has to shorten the variable names) equivalent calls would be:

380 TY = DE:NU = DN:GOSUB 540
420 TY = AD:NU = AN:GOSUB 540
540 REM Routine word using variables TY and NU

Iteration, FOR and REPEAT structures

SuperBASIC uses the conventional FOR ... NEXT loop but can be ended by END FOR rather than NEXT. (In fact both END FOR and NEXT can be used in the same loop but this does not occur in this book.) REPEAT is structurally the same as the BBC's REPEAT ... UNTIL ... except that it ends with an END REPEAT statement. The EXIT statement within a REPEAT loop is the conditional test which ends the loop and does not occur in the END REPeat statement, whereas in BBC BASIC, it does appear as part of the terminating UNTIL statement.

As a REPEAT statement is essentially an endless loop with one or more tests for EXIT conditions it can be simulated by a continuous GOTO loop containing IF ... THEN ... statements which allow leaping out of the loop. Thus the following SuperBASIC fragment:

100 REPeat loop
110 a = a + 1
120 IF a = 10 THEN EXIT loop
130 END REPeat loop

would become in BBC BASIC:

100 REPEAT
110 a = a + 1
120 UNTIL a = 10

and in Spectrum/C64 BASIC:

100 REM Dummy statement for repeat loop
110 a = a + 1
120 IF a = 10 THEN GOTO 140
130 GOTO 100
140 REM next program line

or, more elegantly:

100 REM Dummy statement for repeat loop
110 a = a + 1
120 IF a⟨⟩10 THEN GOTO 100
140 REM next program line

16 THE INTELLIGENT MICRO

SELect ... ON ...
SuperBASIC's SELect statement allows a number of possible choices conditional upon the value of a control variable. Normally it is a way of directing control to one of a choice of procedures. The ON...GOSUB... statement can usually be used in its place. Failing this a series of IF ... THEN ... GOSUBs can replace it, though they will use more lines of program.

INSTR
SuperBASIC contains an INSTR statement which tests to see if a given string is within another. It is similar to the BBC's except for the order of the testing strings. Spectrum and C64 owners will have to write their own routines to do this. The routine must test whether a given substring is within a string and return the position of the first character of the substring if it is found.

Random numbers
The RND function produces numbers in the range specified in the brackets following the function call. Owners of some micros will have to write their own functions to do this and substitute the FN call for the RND call. If RND is followed in a SuperBASIC program by only one number, then the range is between 0 and that number.

Bitwise comparison
In two programs bitwise comparisons are made between bytes of data using bitwise AND and XOR. These are implemented in different ways on different micros. On the QL bitwise AND is represented by && and XOR by ^^.

Recursion
The only area that is likely to prove difficult in conversion to other micros are those two programs in the book which employ recursion. Recursion is a common feature of human intelligence as you will come to see by the time you have finished the book.

A recursive procedure is one which can call itself. QL BASIC and BBC BASIC both employ recursion and there will be no problem in converting all of the programs in this book into BBC BASIC. But the sentence generator and the syllogistic inference program will require some work to adapt for other micros.

Most micros allow subroutines to call themselves, which is the minimum criterion for recursion. So a simple recursive routine would be:

```
100 GOSUB 200
110 t=0
120 END
200 REM Recursive
210 IF t=10 THEN RETURN
220 t=t+1
230 GOSUB 200
240 RETURN
```

This routine will call itself nine times, each time adding 1 to t until it reaches 10, when all the routines will back up.

But recursion is little use unless each 'copy' of the routine has its own variables which are kept intact when other copies of the routine are called. These are normally called local variables because they are local to a particular routine or procedure. They do not exist outside it and cannot be used outside it. In BASIC on the C64 and Spectrum we cannot quite go this far, but we can preserve the variables for each level of a recursive routine by saving them to an array each time a new copy of the routine is called.

This means that an array must previously have been dimensioned with sufficient elements to hold a copy of each of the variables in the routine for each level of recursion that might occur. So if we allow an upper limit of 12 recursions and only to variables in the routine we need an array of 12 × 2 elements. This enables an emulation of recursion as follows:

```
100 DIM v(12,2)
110 a=1:b=1:i=0
120 GOSUB 200
130 END
200 REM Recursive routine
210 IF a+b>23 THEN RETURN
220 i=i+1
230 a=a+1
240 b=b+1
250 PRINT a,b
260 v(i,1)=a:v(i,2)=b:GOSUB 200
270 i=i-1
280 a=v(i,1):b=v(i,2)
290 PRINT a
300 PRINT b
310 RETURN
```

Variable i keeps a record of the level of recursion of the routine and stores a copy of a and b at the appropriate level in the array. The routine, when run, prints firstly ascending then descending numbers.

When the routine is first called a = 1 and b = 1 but 1 is added to each so the number 2 is printed twice at line 250. Then these values are saved to the first level of the array and the routine is called again. The value of i is now 2, 1 is added to a and 1 is added to b, so the numbers 3 and 3 are printed, and these values are saved to the array before the next copy of the routine is called. This continues until the condition in line 210 is met. Then control returns from the lowest level and the earlier values of a and b are given back to them by lines 270 and 280. These values are then printed and control backs up to the next highest value. The previous values are passed to a and b and these are printed, and so on.

The variable i therefore keeps a record of the depth of recursion (like a stack pointer) and a and b, while not local to the routine (because they are the same variables with different values at different levels of recursion rather than different variables with different values) nevertheless control the action at each level of action.

If you find recursion somewhat mind-addling, do not worry—you are not alone. It is a hard concept to get to grips with, especially if you are dealing with emulation on a non-recursive micro. However, without recursion two of the programs in this book will not run as they stand so it is worth trying to master.

3 Creativity

3.1 Creativity basics

Here is another of those impossible questions—what is creativity? No one knows, but it is a key feature of intelligence and one that may prove a major stumbling block if people are ever to produce a human machine. However, as with everything else we will look at in the AI field, there are some limited successes in getting machines to 'create' providing 'creativity' is understood in the widest possible sense. Philosophers and psychologists have never produced a satisfactory account of creativity and this is one of the reasons that the wider term 'intelligence' is so difficult to define. Obviously if a machine is going to act intelligently then it must not simply reproduce what it has learned (or been programmed with) it must use that knowledge to produce new and better solutions to problems and to generate better and more interesting 'ideas' in the areas of its application.

Some people believe that creativity is God-given or impossible to study for some other metaphysical reason, and that attempting to define 'rules' for creativity is therefore a doomed business. This may be so but it seems unlikely, given the gradual successes that have occurred in examining other areas of human psychology which were previously thought too mysterious to be understood by mere mortals. Whether it is true or not, there are certainly theories of creativity and there are, if not rules, then hints and guidelines which can help people come up with solutions to problems, with new ideas and with original thoughts. A well-known practitioner of the art of creative thinking is the psychologist Edward de Bono, who has developed over the years various techniques for 'lateral thinking' and obtaining creative solutions to problems which, while they do not amount to a theory of creativity, nevertheless allow ordinary people to do quite creative things. In other words he has developed a kind of 'heuristics' of creativity, a series of rules of thumb which can help to produce original thoughts. (We will return to the notion of heuristics later in the book.) If we could somehow place these rules of thumb into a computer, then it too should be able to generate ideas of a comparable kind. It seems likely that one development from current work on expert systems (which use rules of thumb, heuristics, for evaluating data) will be systems which can make suggestions using rules like those of de Bono.

We will keep our aims simple, however, and not go too deeply into the realms of theory. Let us just consider one or two kinds of creativity and how we might begin to make a micro come to grips with them. When we talk about creativity normally we generally distinguish at least two kinds: intellectual creativity (the ability to come up with new ideas) and artistic creativity (the ability to create new and pleasing structures in paint, stone, music or words). We will consider both of these but because few micro owners will yet have robot arms capable of carving stone or extensive music synthesizers hooked up to their machines we will look at both kinds of creativity as expressed in words.

The simplest form of verbal creativity is that which linguists usually call 'productivity' (which has nothing to do with how many sentences a linguist has to analyse per hour). Everybody has this kind of creativity in roughly equal measure. It is the ability to produce an infinite number of different sentences using the finite resources of the language. For example, most people only use a vocabulary of a few thousand words (though they know and can understand several thousand more), and those words are spoken using only 45 basic sounds—in English at any rate. So with the finite number of 45 sounds we can produce a huge variety of words, and with only a few thousand words we can all produce and understand an infinite number of sentences. That is to say we can produce a very large number of totally new sentences using a very small finite set of elements.

'QLs are Quite Lovely but BBCs are Better than Blunt Chisels.' Hands up how many people have heard that sentence before? Not many. Neither had I until I typed it. It was probably totally original, but you understood it and so did I and probably everyone reading this book will as well. This is an example of the productivity of English—a limited number of rules and elements can be combined to produce new structures. A very simple example of this is the nursery rhyme 'This is the house that Jack built.' This uses one rule of English to build a complex and potentially infinite structure. The rule says that if you have a relative clause, such as 'that chased the cat' you can add another relative clause to it, e.g., 'that chased the cat that killed the rat'. This is an example of a recursive rule, a rule that can call itself. A relative clause can consist of a relative clause plus a relative clause, which can consist of a relative clause plus a relative clause, which can consist of a relative clause plus a relative clause ... and so on potentially for ever (but the audience would go to sleep). If you want another example of the use of that rule look at the previous sentence.

CREATIVITY

One of the features of QL SuperBASIC, BBC BASIC and a number of other high-level languages like Pascal is that they implement recursion, so a procedure can call itself. Therefore it is possible to add this kind of simple linguistic creativity to any language program written using such languages. Here is a simple example in SuperBASIC:

```
80 CLS
90 PRINT "This is the man";
100 clause
110 STOP
120 DEF PROCedure clause
130 r = RND(10)
140 RESTORE (500 + (r*10))
150 READ noun
160 PRINT "that sat on the";nouns;" ";
170 clause
180 END DEFine clause
500 REMark Data
510 DATA "cat"
520 DATA "dog"
530 DATA "mouse"
540 DATA "man"
550 DATA "elephant"
560 DATA "giraffe"
570 DATA "rat"
580 DATA "rhino"
590 DATA "anteater"
600 DATA "gibbon"
```

(Users of BASICs without recursion should consult Chapter 2 for notes on how to get around the problem.)

When run you will see the micro produce an extremely long sentence using this recursive rule. It goes on much longer than any human being would ever want to. So, if we were using a simple numeric estimate of creativity, we might say that the micro is more creative than you or I in this respect. But this is a very limited kind of creativity and intuitively not very creative at all.

That is because creativity does not simply consist in doing the same thing over and over again. Everybody knows that computers are good at this kind of mechanical repetition and everyone also knows that we usually call such repetition 'mindless', the opposite of intelligent. This is why linguists prefer to call it 'productivity' rather than creativity, though strictly speaking it is creativity of a kind.

A much more interesting kind of creativity involves putting two things together rather than repeating the same thing. Arthur Koestler called this kind of linking of two ideas 'bisociation', by which he means 'bi-association'—the ability to see a relationship between two sets of ideas where previously no one had perceived a connection. A simple example is the famous story of Archimedes. Archimedes had been pondering the problem of how to measure the volume of an irregular solid. He could not find a solution, so went to have a bath to relax. As he entered the bath he saw that the water level rose and he realized that immersing a body in water displaced a volume of water exactly equivalent to the volume of the immersed body. 'Eureka!' He had made the connection between an abstract problem of physics and the mundane activity of having a bath. He had bisociated the two hitherto distinct areas of thought. (And, incidentally, he used the same word for his discovery that we use for computer thought processes—'Eureka' and 'heuristics' are etymologically the same word.)

Though simple, this is quite a powerful theory and, in certain fields, a useful device for producing new ideas. If you want to produce a new idea take an old one and put it next to something totally unrelated, then strive to find a connection between them. Suppose you want to write a new computer game but you have no idea for a scenario. All right, take an old idea, say Space Invaders, put it next to something completely different, say flower arranging, and see what you get—er—how about 'Flower Invaders', a game in which insects have to be kept off the petunias; how about 'Space Arrangers', in which space ships must be used to manoeuvre planets and stars around space to keep the universe balanced; or perhaps the invaders could mutate like flowers, starting off as buds (small and difficult to hit) but gradually growing larger until they begin to shed 'petals' which turn into buds and become more invaders... You see that, if you put your mind to it, ideas can result from the most unlikely combinations. You might even say especially from the most unlikely combinations. Of course, the resulting ideas may be no use. It is one thing to produce ideas and another to produce good ones. Writing a program to do the first job is simplicity itself but the problem of evaluation is much more complex.

3.2 Making a joke

The clearest example of bisociation is in humour. I am not sure if making a joke is intelligent behaviour but it certainly is characteristic human behaviour so any program that makes 'new' jokes could be regarded as human-like. Bisociative programs to do this are elementary. All such a program needs to do is to combine two (more or less) unfunny items together to produce a new item which is funny.

Humour often consists of placing a familiar idea in an unfamiliar context. For example, a common form of humour is to put a powerful, sober or superior human figure in an inappropriate situation. There does not need to be anything humorous about the situation, it simply needs to be inappropriate for such a figure. This is because we tend to stereotype people so that we do not think of judges, for example, as real people who go to the dentist, cut their toenails or get drunk. It is much easier to give them a stereotypical role which is the pompous, erudite and sober image the courts themselves tend to encourage.

The program shown as Fig. 3.1. consists of two lists. One, held as data in lines 310 to 480, is a list of people or types of people whom you are likely to stereotype. The second, lines 490 to 700, is a set of events or situations. Most of them are ordinary though some have a degree of oddity about them. However, you can construct sentences using all of these situations which are not amusing at all. For example, 'a jelly covered in custard' is not amusing (unless your sense of humour is warped), but 'Clive Sinclair covered in custard' is mildly amusing. 'A broken doll sitting in a dustbin' is not amusing. 'Ronald Reagan sitting in a dustbin' is.

The program simply chooses two random numbers. The first is chosen at line 160 and is in the range 0 to 17 because there are 18 people in the first list. The second number is in the range 0 to 21 because there are 22 situations. The numbers defining the upper limits of these ranges are held as the variables anumber and bnumber in case you want to expand the lists.

The program then restores the data pointer to the base line for the list (again abase and bbase can be altered if you add to the lists or change the line numbering) plus the random number, reads in that line and prints it. This is done repeatedly within the loop of lines 140 to 280 until the user decides that enough is enough.

All that we are getting therefore is a random bisociation of items from two lists and, although many of the results are only mildly amusing, it is certainly true that some of the resultant mixtures are amusing and could become the basis of an original joke or TV comedy sketch. It is only a small step from this kind of program to more sophisticated versions which link ideas together in the hope of producing 'original thoughts' or 'discoveries'. The problem with using the bisociative method is that you need very long lists, lots of time

```
100 abase=310
110 bbase=490
120 anumber=17
130 bnumber=21
140 REPeat loop
150 CLS
160 r=RND(anumber)
170 RESTORE ((r*10)+abase)
180 READ parta$
190 AT 1,1:PRINT parta$;" ";
200 r=RND(bnumber)
210 RESTORE ((r*10)+bbase)
220 READ partb$
230 PRINT partb$
240 AT 6,8:PRINT "Any more (Y/N)?"
250 yn$=INKEY$
260 IF yn$="" THEN GO TO 250
270 IF yn$ INSTR "YyNn">2 THEN EXIT loop
280 END REPeat loop
290 PRINT "That´s a funny one"
300 STOP
305 :
310 DATA "a vicar"
320 DATA "a car salesman"
330 DATA "an undertaker"
340 DATA "the prime minister"
350 DATA "a giraffe"
360 DATA "a tax inspector"
370 DATA "a cricketer"
380 DATA "a skinhead"
390 DATA "a computer programmer"
400 DATA "a professor of nuclear physics"
410 DATA "a police sergeant"
420 DATA "the Archbishop of Canterbury"
430 DATA "an oil sheik"
440 DATA "Ronald Reagan"
450 DATA "the author of this book"
460 DATA "a newsreader"
```

Figure 3.1 (*continues*)

```
470 DATA  "Barry Manilow"
480 DATA  "Clive Sinclair"
490 DATA  "wearing only a hat"
500 DATA  "doing a silly walk"
510 DATA  "riding a kangaroo"
520 DATA  "slipping on a banana-skin"
530 DATA  "with purple hair"
540 DATA  "sleeping in a coffin"
550 DATA  "wearing a wig"
560 DATA  "with a patch on one eye"
570 DATA  "talking to a lamppost"
580 DATA  "in love with a tortoise"
590 DATA  "telling jokes to an Eskimo"
600 DATA  "playing Pacman"
610 DATA  "gossiping with Ena Sharples"
620 DATA  "spilling martini on Joan Collins"
630 DATA  "with a bolt through his/her neck"
640 DATA  "riding a hang glider"
650 DATA  "sitting in a dustbin"
660 DATA  "covered in custard"
670 DATA  "doing handstands"
680 DATA  "playing hopscotch"
690 DATA  "singing rude limericks"
700 DATA  "eating soup with a fork"
```

Figure 3.1

and some way of evaluating the output to discard the rubbish. We will re-examine this question when we come to look at expert systems.

3.3 Creating ideas

One drawback with the joke generator is that it is not very creative. It is only putting two things together and these are from clearly defined lists. Although this has some of the characteristics of creativity most people will regard it as limited. A much better program would be one which took more fundamental units and put them together in more complex ways. The basic units of ideas (written ideas at least) are words, so we could say that a sentence generator, in stringing words together in a grammatical way, is creating 'new ideas'. As we will see in the next chapter this is not really the case because ideas depend on meaningful relationships between elements, not just grammatical relationships. So a better idea generator would be one which 'knew' something about the meanings it was putting together. We will pursue this notion later in the book in several different ways. A real idea-generating system would need a high degree of knowledge about meanings. It would need some of the feature-based knowledge discussed in Chapter 7, some ability in creating coherent text as discussed in Chapter 4 and some inferencing or judgement rules as discussed in Chapter 8.

However, we can illustrate the principle of semantic relationships and the idea of using them to build ideas rather than just link two phrases by a short program which creates situations for stories (Fig. 3.2). It was originally developed to produce scenarios for adventure games and, though there are only 90 lines of program and 60 of data it has the capacity to produce many thousands of different ideas. Its main drawback is that many of the ideas are quite stupid. It is not really creative in the human sense because when we say 'creative' we mean 'able to produce good and useful ideas', but it is creative in the sense that it can come up with startlingly original ideas for adventures or fantasy stories, some of which can inspire a human user whose imagination is in the doldrums.

The basis of the program is to have a vocabulary of items that might occur in the fantasy context, each of which is scored according to its meaning. The program simply combines words with appropriate meanings and puts them into sentence-like structures.

Procedure init holds three variables for the number of nouns, adjectives and verbs. The ability of SuperBASIC to support long variable names makes such names eminently clear. Arrays, NA$, AA$ and VA$ are dimensioned to hold the appropriate number of words together with string versions of a numeric code for the meaning. (There is no good reason for holding this numeric information in string arrays except that it keeps all the information together and it is thus easier to remember where everything is.) The extensive data is then read into these arrays, which takes a little time.

The main routine then repeats endlessly until the user breaks into the loop which is generating the ideas. It works by building up noun phrases concerning objects/creatures/beings, then linking two or more such phrases through a verbal relation of some kind. To avoid ungrammatical constructions certain limitations are built into the database and the program, such as using 'THE' rather than 'A' to avoid the problems of agreement. However, most of the possible relations are semantically correct, though some may

```
 10 CLS
 20 init
 30 REPeat loop
 40 PRINT "THE ";
 50 adj
 60 PRINT "THE ";
 70 choose
 80 noun
 90 END REPeat loop
100 STOP
110 :
120 :
130 DEFine PROCedure adj
140 choose
150 R=RND(3)
160 IF R<2 THEN noun:RETURN
170 FOR I=2 TO R
180 REPeat aloop
190 S=RND(adjs)
200 IF AA$(S,2)=NA$(T,2) OR AA$(S,2)="2" THEN EXIT aloop
210 END REPeat aloop
220 length(AA$(S,1))
230 PRINT AA$(S,1);" ";
240 NEXT I
250 noun
260 END DEFine adj
270 :
280 :
290 DEFine PROCedure noun
300 length(NA$(T,1))
310 PRINT NA$(T,1);" ";
320 R=RND(3)
330 IF FLAG <R THEN verb:RETURN
340 PRINT CHR$(8);"."
350 PRINT
360 FLAG = 0
370 END DEFine noun
```

Figure 3.2 (*continues*)

```
380 :
390 :
400 DEFine PROCedure verb
410 REPeat vloop
420 U=RND(verbs)
430 IF VA$(U,2)=NA$(T,2)
    OR VA$(U,2)="2" THEN EXIT vloop
430 END REPeat vloop
440 length(VA$(U,1))
450 PRINT VA$(U,1); " ";
460 FLAG = FLAG +1
470 END DEFine verb
480 :
490 :
500 DEFine PROCedure choose
510 REPeat cloop
520 T=RND(nouns)
530 VV=0
540 IF FLAG <> 0 THEN agree :
    REM CHECK VA AND NA AGREE -
    RETURNS VV=1 IF NOT
550 IF VV<>1 THEN EXIT cloop
560 END REPeat cloop
570 END DEFine choose
580 :
590 :
600 REM Initialisation
610 DEFine PROCedure init
620 nouns = 319
630 adjs = 64
640 verbs = 52
650 DIM NA$(nouns,2,12),AA$(adjs,2,12),
    VA$(verbs,3,12)
660 FLAG=0
670 FOR I=1 TO nouns
680 READ NA$(I,1), NA$(I,2)
690 NEXT I
700 FOR I=1 TO adjs
```

Figure 3.2 *(continues)*

```
710 READ AA$(I,1), AA$(I,2)
720 NEXT I
730 FOR I=1 TO verbs
740 READ VA$(I,1), VA$(I,2), VA$(I,3)
750 NEXT I
760 END DEFine init
770 :
780 :
840 REM CHECK N+V AGREEMENT
850 DEFine PROCedure agree
860 IF VA$(U,3)="2" THEN RETURN
870 IF NA$(T,2)=VA$(U,3) THEN RETURN
880 VV=1
890 END DEFine agree
900 :
910 :
920 DATA "HOUSE",0,"DRAGON",1,"TROLL",1,
    "GOBLIN",1,"KEY",0
930 DATA "STONE",0,"BOOK",0,"SCROLL",0,
    "POTION",0,"SLAVE",1
940 DATA "HAT",0,"COAT",0,"CLOAK",0,
    "BOOTS",0,"BAG",0
950 DATA "GAUNTLETS",0,"ROBE",0,
    "HELMET",0,"CROWN",0
960 DATA "EARRINGS",0,"RING",0,
    "NECKLACE",0,"CHAIN",0
970 DATA "SCARF",0,"SHAWL",0,"ARMLET",0,
    "BRACELET",0
980 DATA "TORQUE",0,"JACKET",0,"TUNIC",0,
    "TROUSERS",0
990 DATA "BELT",0,"POUCH",0,"SACK",0,
    "SANDALS",0,"ANKLET",0,"DRESS",0
1000 DATA "HELM",0,"CHAINMAIL",0,
    "ARMOUR",0,"GREAVES",0
1010 DATA "VANBRACES",0,"BREASTPLATE",0,
    "SHIELD",0,"BUCKLER",0,"SPURS",0
1020 DATA "DAGGER",0,"SWORD",1,"MACE",0,
    "HAMMER",0
```

Figure 3.2 (*continues*)

```
1030 DATA "FLAIL",0,"SPEAR",0,"JAVELIN",0,
     "MORNING STAR",0
1040 DATA "BOW",0,"ARROW",0,"SLING",0,
     "CROSSBOW",0,"PIKE",0,"LANCE",0,
     "DART",0
1050 DATA "WEAPON",0,"CLUB",0,"STAFF",0,
     "WAND",1,"SCIMITAR",0
1060 DATA "TRIDENT",0,"HALBERD",0,
     "AXE",0,"PICKAXE",0,"JERKIN",0,
     "WHIP",0,"QUARREL",0
1070 DATA "SCABBARD",0,"QUIVER",0,"CAP",0,
     "WIG",0,"GLOVES",0
1080 DATA "WINESKIN",0,"TINDERBOX",0,
     "TORCH",0,"SPIKE",0,"BOAT",0,
     "POLE",0
1090 DATA "MIRROR",1,"LANTERN",0,
     "CHEST",0,"MAP",0,"SCROLLCASE",0
1100 DATA "CANDLE",0,"PACK",0,"BEADS",0,
     "CROSS",0,"FLASK",0,"SADDLE",0,
     "BLANKET",0
1110 DATA "CART",0,"HERB",0,"TREE",1,
     "FOOD",0,"BEER",0,"BREAD",0,
     "APPLE",0,"WINE",0
1120 DATA "MEAT",0,"CHICKEN",1,"COW",1,
     "DOG",1,"DONKEY",1,"GOAT",1,"HAWK",1
1130 DATA "HORSE",1,"MULE",1,"OX",1,
     "PIGEON",1,"PIG",1
1140 DATA "SHEEP",1,"BIRD",1,"EAGLE",1,
     "SWAN",1,"SQUIRREL",1,"SPARROW",1
1150 DATA "DUCK",1,"FERRET",1,"CAT",1,
     "BEAR",1,"WOLF",1,"FOX",1,"LION",1,
     "TIGER",1
1160 DATA "APE",1,"ANT",1,"BADGER",1,
     "BANDIT",1,"BANSHEE",1
1170 DATA "BASILISK",1,"BEAVER",1,
     "BEETLE",1,"BERSERKER",1,"DRAGON",1,
     "BOAR",1,"BROWNIE",1
1180 DATA "BUGBEAR",1,"BULL",1
```

Figure 3.2 (*continues*)

```
1190 DATA "CAVEMAN",1,"CENTAUR",1,
     "CENTIPEDE",1,"CHIMERA",1,
     "COCKATRICE",1,"CRAB",1
1200 DATA "CROCODILE",1,"DEMON",1,
     "DEVIL",1,"DINOSAUR",1,"GENIE",1,
     "DRYAD",1,"DWARF",1
1210 DATA "ELEMENTAL",1,"MAN",1,"EEL",1,
     "ELEPHANT",1,"ELF",1,"WOMAN",1,
     "GIRL",1,"BOY",1,"CHILD",1
1220 DATA "BABY",1,"FAIRY",1,"FAWN",1,
     "DEER",1,"FROG",1,"STAG",1,
     "FUNGUS",1,"GARGOYLE,1
1230 DATA "GHOST",1,"GHOUL",1,"GIANT",1,
     "GNOLL",1,"GNOME",1,"GOBLIN",1,
     "GOLEM",1,"GORGON",1,"SLIME",1,
     "GRIFFON",1,"HALFLING",1,"HARPY",1,
     "HOUND",1,"HOBGOBLIN",1,"HAWK",1,
     "HYDRA",1
1240 DATA "OGRE",1,"KOBOLD",1,"INSECT",1,
     "LEOPARD",1,"LICH",1,"LIZARD",1,
     "LIZARDMAN",1,"LURKER",1,WEREBEAR",1,
     "WEREWOLF",1,"WERERAT",1
1250 DATA "MANTICORE",1,"MEDUSA",1,
     "MERMAN",1,"MERMAID",1,"MINOTAUR",1,
     "MOULD",1,"MOLE",1,"MUMMY",1,"NAGA",1,
     "SPIRIT",1,"NIXIE",1,"NOMAD",1,
     "NYMPH",1
1260 DATA "ORC",1,"MAGE",1,"OWL",1,
     "PEGASUS",1,"PIERCER",1,"PIRATE",1,
     "MAGE",1,"SORCERER",1,"RAT",1,
     "ROCK",0,"MONSTER",1,"SALAMANDER",1,
     "SATYR",1,"PIXY",1
1270 DATA
     "SCORPION",1,"SHADOW",1,
     "SKELETON",1,"SLUG",1,"SNAKE",1,
     "SPECTRE",1,"SPIDER",1,"SPRITE",1,
     "STIRGE",1,"SYLPH",1,"TOAD",1
1280 DATA "ENT",1,"OAK",1,"TROLL",1,
```

Figure 3.2 (*continues*)

```
          "SOLDIER",1,"UNICORN",1,"VAMPIRE",1,
          "WASP",1,"BUSH,0,FERRET",1,"WIGHT",1,
          "WRAITH",1,"WYVERN",1,"ZOMBIE",1
1290 DATA "RIVER",0,"SEA",0,"POND",0,
          "LAKE",0,"WATERFALL",0,"ISLAND",0,
          "FORD",0,"STREAM",0,"OCEAN",0,
          "MOUNTAIN",0,"HILL",0,"STONE",0,
          "CLIFF",0,"RAVINE",0
1300 DATA "CITADEL",0,"PALACE",0,"CITY",0,
          "CAVE",0,"VILLAGE",0,"FARM",0,
          "FORTRESS",0,"FOREST",0,"TOWER",0,
          "HUT",0,"CASTLE",0
1310 DATA "GLADE",0,"WOOD",0,"TOWN",0,
          "GLACIER",0,"RIDGE",0
1320 DATA "THIEF",1,"WIZARD",1,"KING",1,
          "QUEEN",1,"PRINCE",1,"KNIGHT",1,
          "SORCERER",1,"FIGHTER",1,"CLERIC",1,
          "DRUID",1,"PALADIN",1,"ASSASSIN",1
1330 DATA "SORCERESS",1,"NURSE",1,
          "PRINCESS",1,"RANGER",1,"BARD",1,
          "INNKEEPER",1,"SMITH",1,"COOPER",1,
          "DOCTOR",1,"MIDWIFE",1,"WITCH",1
1340 DATA "MERCHANT",1,"FARMER",1,
          "WOODSMAN",1,"HUNTER",1,"FURRIER",1,
          "BOOK",0,"AMBASSADOR",1
1350 DATA "COOK",1,"SAILOR",1,"GUARD",1,
          "MAN AT ARMS",1,"OSTLER",1,"GROOM",1,
          "PEASANT",1
1360 DATA "COLD",2,"STUPID",1,"STEEL",0,
          "GOLD",2,"COPPER",0
1370 DATA "BLACK",2,"BLUE",2,"WHITE",2,
          "GREEN",2,"YELLOW",2,"RED",2,
          "ORANGE",2,"PURPLE",2,"SILVER",2,
          "BRONZE",0
1380 DATA "INTELLIGENT",2,"CLEVER",2,
          "IRON",2,"WOODEN",0,"RUBY",0,
          "SAPPHIRE",0,"TOPAZ",0,"JET",0,
          "IVORY",0,"MOONSTONE",0,"OPAL",0
```

Figure 3.2 (*continues*)

```
1390 DATA "AMETHYST",0,"AGATE",0,
     "GARNET",0,"TURQUOISE",0,"CRAZY",1,
     "LAZY",1,"SILLY",1,"BROKEN",0,"HOT",2,
     "ICY",2,"FIERY",2,"UNDEAD",1
1400 DATA "GRANITE",0,"HARD",2,"SOFT",2,
     "GENTLE",1,"STERN",1,"COMFORTABLE",0,
     "STRONG",1,"WEAK",1,"UGLY",2,
     "ATTRACTIVE",2
1410 DATA "WOUNDED",1,"HEALTHY",1,"ILL",1,
     "MAD",1,"PERFECT",2,"ANCIENT",2,
     "DAMAGED",0,"FRIGHTENING",2,
     "WORRIED",1
1420 DATA "HOLY",2,"WICKED",1,"EVIL",2,
     "FURTIVE",1,"DRUNKEN",1,"HUNGRY",1,
     "DECEITFUL",1
1430 DATA "KEPT IN",0,0,"FOUND NEAR",2,0,
     "POISONED BY",1,1,
     "MADE BY",0,1,
     "MAKER OF",1,0,"ENEMY OF",1,1,
     "POSSESSED BY",0,1
1440 DATA "ENEMY OF",1,1,
     "HATED BY", 2,1, "PURSUING",1,1,
     "CONCEALING",2,2
1450 DATA "MAKER OF",1,0,
     "MADE BY",0,1,"OWNED BY",2,1,
     "GIVEN TO",0,1,"TAKEN FROM",2,1
1480 DATA "CHASED BY",1,1,
     "DISCOVERED BY",2,1,"HIDDEN BY",2,2,
     "FRIEND OF",1,1,"PROTECTOR OF",1,2,
     "ASSASSIN OF",1,1,"RULER OF",1,2,
     "HOME OF",0,1
1490 DATA "LIVING WITH",1,2,
     "SLAVE OF",1,1,"HIDING FROM",1,1,
     "RUNNING FROM",1,1,"RUNNING TO",1,2,
     "LOVED BY",2,1,"STOLEN FROM",2,2
1500 DATA "CAUGHT BY",1,1,
     "CAUGHT WITH",1,2,"SERVANT OF",1,1,
     "MASTER OF",1,2,"WORSHIPPED BY",2,1,
```

Figure 3.2 (*continues*)

```
              "FOUND NEAR",2,2
    1510 DATA "VALUED BY",2,1,
              "LOST NEAR",2,0,"LOST BY",2,1,
              "FRIEND OF",1,1,"CONQUERER OF",1,1,
              "ENCHANTED BY",2,2,"BEARER OF",1,0
```
Figure 3.2

seem a little odd. The basis of this correctness is the numbers held in the DATA statements after each word or phrase. All nouns and adjectives have a single number code; all verb phrases have two number codes. Code 0 means that the word is inanimate, 1 means that it is animate and 2 means that it could be either. The verb phrases have two codes because they are preceded by a word that may be animate or inanimate as well as followed by the same choice. So the phrase 'hated by' must be followed by an animate phrase because only animate things can hate, but may be preceded by either an animate or an inanimate phrase as both classes of thing can be hated. Its code is therefore '2,1'.

The program simply selects a noun phrase, then a verb phrase, then another noun phrase. However, each noun phrase can have up to three adjectives and a noun phrase may itself consist of an embedded verb phrase plus noun phrase. (A different way to approach this would be to make these procedures recursive, but I have opted for the clearer method here.) So an elementary selection would be a simple noun phrase plus a verb phrase plus another simple noun phrase, all of them agreeing and none using adjectives, such as:

THE PRINCESS + IN LOVE WITH + THE FROG.

The next most complex version adds one or more adjectives, such as:

THE GIANT MUSHROOM BROKEN BY THE UGLY BLACK GOBLIN.

Finally the most complex is one which modifies the final noun phrase by adding a verb phrase to it, such as:

THE STONE HELMET WORN BY THE GREEN DRAGON FEARED BY THE ANCIENT CLEVER WIZARD.

Of course for every idea that makes reasonable sense you will still find quite a number which are nonsensical, funny or impossible. If you wanted to reduce these you would have to build in other types of semantic constraint in addition to the test for animacy. The kinds of things you might test for could be size, mobility, whether they can be eaten or not, whether they have emotions, etc. This is termed a feature-based analysis and is discussed later in the book. There is a huge number of possible relations such an analysis could work upon and every one you add to the program will reduce the inventiveness of the ideas and will have some exceptions which make the rule difficult to apply.

Perhaps you can begin to see why making a computer intelligent is such a difficult task. Just to make it understand the word 'SACK', for example, means that it has to know a sack is floppy unless something is in it, that it can be moved, but only if an animate thing is moving it (unless the inanimate thing is actually a force such as the wind or the tide), that it is a container, that it is not a house in the human sense but that things can live in it, that it can be cut and torn, that it can leak but not hold liquids . . . and so on. You can imagine how difficult it would be to program all the knowledge required to use language properly even in a very limited area. Nevertheless it is fun trying.

You could also try adapting the program by providing different databases which could be used for other types of plot or scenario, such as Science Fiction or Western. Other databases, rather more remote from the type usually found in an adventure game, could include different kinds of human social or political relationships, or the kinds of relations typical of TV soap opera, or any situation where two elements are linked in some way. In principle any simple domain in which ideas can be generated more or less 'mechanically' by linking two hitherto remote concepts could be incorporated into a program such as this.

3.4 Improving the idea generator

You can probably see from this that any real 'creativity' here comes from the user rather than the program. The user creates the database and the user evaluates the results. It is the user who interprets the program's output and if the user cannot apply the output to the desired task then no creativity has occurred at all. The program is therefore really a tool for creating new phrases, new links between words. It is the user who finds the usefulness (or not) of the ideas behind those words. This is actually quite close to part of the processes of some human creativity. Very often people will have ideas which they change, alter, mature and evaluate before using them, and the original source of the 'idea' can be very remote from the final solution. Thus the program really serves to spark the imagination rather than to replace it. It throws up unlimited suggestions in the hope that sooner or later something will occur that the user can make sense of.

The principle could probably be extended. One could imagine a program which operated a number of the rules for lateral thinking popularized by psychologists like Edward de Bono. Much of his work shows that people fail to find solutions to problems because they get trapped in particular patterns of thinking and find it impossible to enter into a different mode of thought. If we had a program which, as a matter of course, simply applied all the possible strategies to a particular idea, this should create a number of suggestions which, however absurd, suggest to the user more sensible variants that break the restricting thought pattern in which the problem solver is trapped. (If you can write such a program then you are probably made for life!)

If we wanted such a program to be more useful we would want one or two additional features. First we would want the ideas generated to be more relevant to a specific problem or project, and secondly we would want some degree of evaluation of the ideas so that some of the rubbish is not produced or, if produced, is not offered to the user. To obtain the first we would have to seed the database with relevant information. For example if we were looking for ways of improving productivity in an assembly line for producing cars we would restrict the vocabulary to words like 'fewer', 'more', 'slower', 'faster', 'robots', 'cars', 'workers', 'teabreaks', etc. It would be a good idea also if the user could create such a vocabulary which means putting a 'front end' on the program which takes the user through the task of defining the problem area and selecting the crucial vocabulary. At the same time there are probably a number of concepts such as 'more', 'cheaper', and 'attractive' which could be a permanent part of such a database because they would be relevant to a majority of problems. In addition to this we would want ideas which were more sophisticated than simply placing a noun and an adjective next to each other and therefore we would want rules for stringing bits of ideas together in an extended way in order to produce more complex suggestions. For example one rule for a complex idea might be:

ADJECTIVE + NOUN + LINK   PHRASE + ADJ + NOUN   (+   LINK PHRASE + ADJ + NOUN), etc.

where link phrases would be things like 'but not', 'as well as', 'without', 'alternating with', and so on.

Such a program would work better with some problem areas than with others. Producing a worthwhile version of this program would involve many more complexities than we can examine here, but if you want to make the attempt the key to producing a successful program of this kind is to have as clear an idea of the problem area as you can and as full a database as you can. Do not exclude things you can think of no interesting ideas for—these may be the very areas that you are stuck in and which the program can explore for new relationships.

The second requirement, for a degree of self-evaluation, would be very difficult to implement. There are really two aspects to human creativity—the productive side and the interpretative side. It seems likely that machines will eventually be able to mimic much of the productive side by using strategies discovered in human creativity such as bisociation. But interpretation is a very different matter. It lies at the heart of one branch of AI, namely pattern recognition. In order to get a machine to 'see' or to 'hear' or to 'understand speech' it has to be able to recognize patterns in the data presented to it. That is, it has to be able to turn raw data into meaningful information. Computers are good at handling raw data and at producing it, but they are pretty stupid when it comes to interpretation.

Interpretation involves selecting from a mass of available data all and only the data that is useful and/or relevant. This means that the machine needs to know what that data is relevant to and what it is meant to be useful for. This is the problem of defining context and it is a problem which we have very little understanding of. Even the major practical success of AI, the expert system, has little use in areas where humans do not understand their own expertise, where the expert himself cannot define what he is doing or how he selects relevant and useful information. Indeed a whole new kind of human expert has arisen to cope with this problem. The 'knowledge engineer' has the task of extracting from human beings all the complexity of their expertise even when they themselves cannot describe or explain it.

So any ideas you have in this area may well be original and if you write a program incorporating them it is likely to be an original program. There are some strategies we could use for making an ideas generator self-evaluative, but they are of limited value and they may well remove the most interesting ideas. One tactic would be to get the user to define what he means by 'good idea' in such a way that only ideas fitting that definition would be kept by the program. Suppose that each concept added to the database was scored by the user according to its importance in the problem area. For example, our car manufacturer might regard 'workers' as the most important concept, giving a high score (say 9) but the gender of the workers, whilst a relevant variable, might have only a low score because not very important (say 2). Similarly relationships like 'cheaper than' might be scored highly (say 8) but 'labour saving' might be lower (say 3). The program could then be instructed to report only on ideas it produced which had a total score above 18. If this produced no satisfactory results the threshold could be lowered—more ridiculous ideas would result but there is a greater likelihood of something useful turning up.

A second approach would be to give the ideas ranking according to their complexity. For example, each concept could be scored according to its 'problem value' in the estimation of the user, each relationship could be scored for 'simplicity' and each idea could additionally be scored for the number of concepts and/or relations it used, with the greater number indicating greater complexity. This means that the user would need to do a fair amount of introspecting to decide what scores to use (is machinery that is prone to break down more problematic than staff that are prone to sickness and strike?) but would have the advantage that ideas could be offered with a rating as to their usefulness (how problematic the units are, how simple the relationships are and how complex the overall idea is).

It would also be possible to combine both approaches, but this adds more burden to the user and involves the programmer in a balancing of values because it would be necessary to decide whether complexity was more significant in estimating the value of an idea than the user's estimate of the importance of the individual components. The difficulties of such an approach are not insuperable, however. Nevertheless, even a complex approach of this kind would not involve much in the way of determining relevance. You could even argue that in scoring all the concepts and relations him- or herself the user was actually doing all the work and the program would simply show the user what he or she already knows. While this is true it is not very helpful. One of the major difficulties faced by people in trying to solve problems or to come up with new ideas is being trapped in a particular subset of the information available to them. Such a program would be a way of helping the user 'realize' what he or she knows and break out of that trap.

4 Artistic creativity

4.1 But is it art?

We have discussed intellectual creativity. Now we want to examine what might be involved in getting a machine to do something artistic. It is probably true that each kind of artistic endeavour has its own special properties. Obviously there are certain very special skills involved in each type of art. Painters and sculptors need particular kinds of manual dexterity and perceptual abilities, composers need a knowledge of music, the ability to hear pure pitch and the ability to play music, writers need a command of a language, a large vocabulary and a knowledge of literary conventions.

However, none of these things in themselves makes someone creative. You could say that these are skills necessary for artistic creativity but not sufficient for it.

Even so, many people argue that artistic creativity is no more than the application of a series of rules in exactly the same way that linguistic productivity is the application of rules. The difference is that artistic creativity involves more rules, more complex rules and a large number of interrelations between rules, and might include such paradoxes as 'rules for how and when to break other rules' and 'rules for disobeying the rules'. What we might conclude from this debate is that computers can be creative if programmers and designers can ensure three things:

1. The computer has to be given, or given control of, skills equivalent to those used by its human counterpart. For example, robot arms must be able to manipulate paintbrushes with the same degree of accuracy as a Leonardo, or screen resolutions and colours must be as variable as a pointillist painting.
2. The rules for a particular kind of creativity must be discovered. For example, what is it that makes a poet write 'To be or not to be' rather than 'to exist or to cease to exist'?
3. The discovered rules must be expressed in a way that a computer can employ them. For example, a musician might say 'I begin by thinking of rhythm and that always suggests a melody' but this would be a rather difficult rule to give to a computer.

You will have realized what is coming next... computers can have a degree of creativity to the extent that the above three conditions can be met. Let us take literature as a test case. In order to get a computer to write a story or a poem it must have some basic skills of language. We will be looking at these in more detail in a later chapter but for the moment all we need to say is that 'knowing a language' is quite a complex business. At its simplest it involves knowing the alphabet (and the sounds of the language) and how to string those letters or sounds into words, and knowing a large number of words, and how to string those into sentences, and knowing how to string sentences together to make texts. But there are a number of intermediate stages and there are all sorts of oddities in real (or 'natural') language. Consider as an example the relation between the English spelling system and the English sound system. How do you teach a computer that the 'ough' represents different sounds in 'rough', 'through', 'although', and 'bough'? But if you cannot do this, how can you teach a computer about rhyme?

A great deal of energy has been devoted to discovering the rules of language. Everybody knows them, of course, otherwise we would not be able to use a language, but very few people can say what they know. The result has been that many of the rules of language production are known sufficiently well for passable sentence-generating programs to exist (providing the computer has enough memory and the programmer has enough patience for all the rules). A simple sentence producer is given below. It uses a grammar of the following form:

1. Sentence = noun phrase + verb phrase
2. noun phrase = determiner (+ adjective string) + noun
3. adjective string = adjective (+ adjective string)
4. verb phrase = verb + noun phrase (+ adverb)
5. adjective = [big, small, black, white, cheap, expensive, light, heavy]
6. adverb = [quickly, slowly, yesterday, today, reluctantly, cheekily]
7. noun = [man, woman, boy, girl, programmer, salesperson, designer, author, reader]
8. determiner = [a, the]
9. verb = [scolded, angered, offended, persuaded, reminded, annoyed, helped, rewarded, befriended]

A grammar is almost a primitive program when it is written like this. These rules are called 'rewrite rules' and you should read them in the following way: '=' means 'is rewritten as', '( )' means 'is optional' and '[ ]' means 'choose one of'. So a sentence can be rewritten as a noun phrase plus a verb phrase; a noun phrase can be rewritten as a determiner plus an optional adjective string plus a noun; a noun is one of the items in brackets. Notice that we have another example of a recursive rule here. The adjective string consists of an adjective plus an optional adjective string, which consists of an adjective plus an adjective string ... and so on. Language is full of recursive rules of this kind, which is one of the reasons why writing language-producing programs can be expensive on memory.

4.2 Sentence generator

A sentence generator based on the above grammar is given in Fig. 4.1. If you examine and RUN this program you will notice several things. Firstly the structure of the program is very close to the grammar on which it is based. This is a characteristic of language-processing programs—good programs represent grammars of the chosen language, making it very easy to see exactly what a given program can and cannot do.

This has been deliberately exploited to make the methods clearer, and

```
100 r=4
110 RANDOMISE
120 CLS
130 noun=610:no_no=9
140 verb=730:ve_no=10
150 adjective=850:adj_no=5
160 adverb=930:adv_no=5
170 determiner=1000:de_no=4
180 REPeat loop
190 CLS
200 PRINT
210 sentence
220 PRINT
230 AT 10,8:PRINT "Another sentence (Y/N)?"
240 REPeat inloop
250 yn$=INKEY$:IF yn$="" THEN GO TO 250
260 IF yn$ INSTR "YyNn" THEN EXIT inloop
270 END REPeat inloop
280 IF yn$ INSTR "Nn" THEN EXIT loop
290 END REPeat loop
300 STOP
```

Figure 4.1 (*continues*)

```
310 :
320 DEFine PROCedure sentence
330 noun_phrase
340 verb_phrase
350 END DEFine sentence
360 :
370 DEFine PROCedure noun_phrase
380 word determiner,de_no
390 ad = RND(4)
400 REPeat adloop
410 IF ad <2 THEN EXIT adloop
420 word adjective,adj_no
430 ad=ad-1
440 END REPeat adloop
450 word noun,no_no
460 END DEFine noun_phrase
470 :
480 DEFine PROCedure verb_phrase
490 word verb,ve_no
500 noun_phrase
510 word adverb,adv_no
520 END DEFine verb_phrase
530 :
540 DEFine PROCedure word(type,number)
550 r=RND(number)
560 RESTORE (type+(10*r))
570 READ word$
580 PRINT word$;" ";
590 END DEFine word
600 :
610 REMark Nouns
620 DATA "MAN"
630 DATA "CAT"
640 DATA "WOMAN"
650 DATA "PROGRAMMER"
660 DATA "BOY"
670 DATA "GIRL"
680 DATA "DESIGNER"
```

Figure 4.1 *(continues)*

```
690  DATA "AUTHOR"
700  DATA "ASSISTANT"
710  DATA "ROBOT"
720  :
730  REMark Verbs
740  DATA "ANNOYED"
750  DATA "PLEASED"
760  DATA "ANGERED"
770  DATA "REWARDED"
780  DATA "HELPED"
790  DATA "PLEASED"
800  DATA "DISPLEASED"
810  DATA "SCOLDED"
820  DATA "PERSUADED"
830  DATA "OFFENDED"
840  :
850  REMark Adjectives
860  DATA "BORING"
870  DATA "STUPID"
880  DATA "BRILLIANT"
890  DATA "WORRYING"
900  DATA "HUMOROUS"
910  DATA "CLEVER"
920  :
930  REMark Adverbs
940  DATA "YESTERDAY"
950  DATA "TODAY"
960  DATA "GREATLY"
970  DATA "SOMETIMES"
980  DATA "EVENTUALLY"
990  :
1000 REMark Determiners
1010 DATA "A"
1020 DATA "THE"
1030 DATA "ANOTHER"
1040 DATA "THAT"
```

Figure 4.1

SuperBASIC facilitates a high degree of 'natural' expression in describing such things as a grammar of a language. You can see, for example, that the whole generating procedure is hierarchical, just as language is a holistic structure of patterns at different levels. The main program simply consists of one call—sentence. All the other procedures are subprocedures of this procedure. Lines 100 to 200 simply declare the necessary variables and control the display. Lines 220 to 290 likewise control display and the possible printing of additional sentences. Other BASICs may of course use subroutines rather than procedures but the principle remains the same.

Procedure sentence itself consists of two parts, like any simple sentence—a noun phrase and a verb phrase, each its own procedure. Noun phrase consists of a series of calls to procedure word with parameters representing the area of the dictionary that the word is to be drawn from and the maximum number of items in that part of the dictionary. Firstly it looks for a determiner, so procedure word produces a random number in the range fixed by the actual parameter (i.e., in this case de__no). It then restores the data pointer to that line number (the method we have already used in earlier programs) and reads in the word which will be A, THE, ANOTHER or THAT. The word is then printed.

Then the number of adjectives in this noun phrase is randomly chosen (line 390) and a loop repeated that number of times, each time calling the word-printing procedure with parameters that result in the printing of adjectives. Finally procedure word is called to print a noun.

Procedure verb__phrase operates in the same manner. Firstly it selects a verb, using procedure word, then it calls procedure noun__phrase, which carries out the stages we have just outlined, and then it prints an adverb using procedure word again.

Arguably this is how a human being goes about constructing a sentence of this form—using each high-order structure in order and working through the tree which realizes that structure before moving on to the next structure at the same level. Of course, at the highest level there is the choice of meaning which affects all lower choices, but we have not considered it here.

You will also see that the program can be expanded without much alteration. There are two kinds of expansion. One is simply to add words to the vocabulary. The start line of each vocabulary class and the number of items in that class is declared in the opening lines of the program. Add your new words by extending the appropriate block of data statements and alter the two relevant declarations accordingly.

If you try this expansion of vocabulary, however, you will quicky realize the third aspect of the problem and consequently the other possible direction for expansion. The vocabulary listed here is very restricted. If you begin to add nouns like 'cat', 'beauty' or 'crowds', or verbs like 'inhabits', 'thinks' or 'wishes' or adverbs like 'tomorrow', 'easily' or 'at once' nonsense sentences will quickly result, such as 'A crowds thinks a beauty at once'. Clearly this is not a complete grammar of English but it can be added to to make it more versatile and capable of wider types of vocabulary.

For example, two extra rules might be:

10. noun phrase = noun phrase + prepositional phrase
11. prepositional phrase = preposition + noun phrase
12. preposition = [to,with,by]

This is another rule set using recursion, and it permits the addition of phrases like 'with the computer', 'by the man with the robot' and so on. To incorporate it within the program we alter procedure noun__phrase so that a random number determines whether a prepositional phrase occurs and if it does then a new procedure, PROC prep__phrase, is called.

```
DEF PROCedure prep__phrase
word preposition,pe__no
noun__phrase
END DEFine prep__phrase
```

In addition the prepositions must be added to the data and the start line of the block (preposition) together with the number of prepositions (pe__no) must be declared. Suppose we wanted to add conjunctions so that sentences could be linked together. Then we must change the first rule to: Sentence = noun phrase + verb phrase (+ conjunction + sentence). This can be implemented by adding another random choice at the beginning of the program and repeated calls to a conjunction-writing procedure and to the procedure 'sentence' made accordingly.

You can continue in the same way for as long as you like. Auxiliary verbs could be added, tense could be changed, relative clauses could be added, provision could be made for the choice of pronouns (I, you, we) and proper nouns (Noel, Clive Sinclair, London) and a number of other modifications could be made. However, if you do intend to write a sentence-producing program of this kind I would not recommend that you proceed in this way except in order to discover the limitations of your model and programming. Because of the close correspondence between grammars and programs it is much better to write a complete grammar of the types of sentence you wish to produce before you begin program design and certainly before you begin coding. We will consider two other approaches to grammars and language programming in later chapters, which will help you to decide what limitations you will settle for in a language-producing program.

4.3 Creating poetry

Let us move on now to one really creative task—writing literature. Surely a computer will not ever be able to produce masterpieces? At the moment this is certainly true. However, as researchers clarify the nature of certain literary tasks so they begin to become programmable. Computers can write primitive stories. They are not very entertaining but they have many of the features we recognize as belonging to stories. Computers can also paraphrase other stories (i.e., recognize the essential elements of a real story) and summarize the causal strings that form the plot of many stories. Work by Schank, Abelson and others has produced many programs written in LISP which are able to produce and to 'comprehend' in different but limited ways the nature of narrative and other kinds of text, because Schank has been able to describe rules which, if they are not the ones humans actually use, nevertheless accurately represent what people know.

An example of the story-producing program is TALE-SPIN which generates stories like: 'Once upon a time Fred Fox lived near a pond. There was a hole in the ground. Monty Mole lived in the hole in the ground. Monty Mole was thirsty. Fred Fox was a friend of Monty Mole. Fred Fox went to the pond. Fred Fox got some water. Fred Fox went to the hole in the ground. Fred Fox gave the water to Monty Mole. Monty Mole was not thirsty any more.' This is not a transcript of output from TALE-SPIN, which would actually include much more redundancy, but it ably shows both how close to and how far from truly entertaining narratives current AI research is.

Similarly we cannot yet get computers to write sophisticated poetry, but we can obtain verse of sorts by specifying the constraints (the literary rules) which a particular verse form embodies. One of the simplest verse forms is the rhyming couplet. Two lines of verse are put side by side, each with the same number of stresses and ending with words having the same sound. This looks like a pair of rules that a computer could be given and work with, so let us examine a simple verse generator.

If we were going to do things thoroughly we would have a dictionary of possible words (like the dictionary used in the previous program) and against each word there would be a representation of its stress pattern. Then the program would construct two grammatical sentences which held words with the total number of required stresses (for the sake of argument we will say four stresses) and ending in words that rhyme. This would be a rhyming couplet.

However, this is not even as easy as it sounds because we have ignored the fundamental problem, that of meaning. The whole point about language is that it strings elements together to give meaning. So it would not be enough simply to produce grammatical, evenly stressed rhyming sentences, as there is no guarantee either that the individual sentences would be meaningful or that the two sentences would be semantically connected. We will return to the vexed question of semantics later in the book, but for the moment we will use a little sleight of hand to get round it.

Suppose that we identified a small set of subjects ('meanings', if you like) that were commonly used in poetry and constructed a database for our poetry generator which did not have words as its elements but meaningful phrases, each of which was something to do with one of these subjects. If we made each phrase two stresses long then any four phrases would make a couplet providing:

1. the second phrase and the fourth phrase ended with the same sound;
2. each phrase connected with the preceding phrase in an acceptable manner.

This is the approach used in Versificator (Fig. 4.2). The database contains phrases about four subject areas which are common subjects in poetry— nature, life, love and time. If you look at Shakespeare's Sonnets, for example, you will find that almost all of them involve more than one of these themes. Each phrase has only two stresses, though the stresses are not placed at the same position in each phrase and there are unequal numbers of unstressed syllables.

Almost all the phrases could stand on their own successfully, i.e., they are complete sentences, so to achieve some measure of coherence our couplet could at a pinch simply be made up of four short sentences, though this is not the approach used in the program. Finally all the phrases are grouped into rhyming sets, i.e., there are more than two phrases ending in each sound. This ensures that whatever phrase is chosen as the second in our four-phrase structure there will be a choice of at least two to rhyme with it. (Our verse is going to be very boring if the same two phrases are always chosen for a particular rhyme.)

An important feature of rhyme, however, remains to be discussed. Rhyme involves similarity of sound. How then can a computer (without acoustic sensors) recognize rhyme? The answer is once again that it cannot, but a combination of rules and a carefully chosen database will enable it to do so.

```
100 no_of_statements=53
110 CLS
120 T=RND(1 TO 4)
130 FOR J=1 TO T
140 FOR i=1 TO 3
150   choose
160   IF i=2 THEN rhyme$=syllable$:
      key$=phrase$:the:PRINT:PRINT"                ";
170   IF i=3 THEN PRINT
180   PRINT phrase$;
190 NEXT i
200 REPeat loop
210   choose
220   IF rhyme$=syllable$ AND key$<>phrase$
      THEN EXIT loop
230 END REPeat loop
240 the
250 PRINT
260 PRINT "              ";phrase$;"."
270 NEXT J
280 STOP
290 :
300 DEFine FuNction syllable$
310   pattern$=
      phrase$(LEN(phrase$)-1 TO LEN (phrase$))
320   RETurn pattern$
330 END DEFine syllable$
340 :
350 DEFine PROCedure choose
360   r=RND(no_of_statements)
370   RESTORE ((r*10)+540)
380   READ phrase$
390 END DEFine choose
400 :
410 DEFine PROCedure the
420   s=RND(5)
430   IF phrase$(1 TO 3)<>"THE" OR s=1
      THEN PRINT ", ";:RETurn
440   SELect ON s
```

Figure 4.2 (*continues*)

```
450 ON s=2
460 phrase$=" AS" &
    phrase$(4 TO LEN(phrase$))
470 ON s=3
480 phrase$=" LIKE"
    & phrase$(4 TO LEN(phrase$))
490 ON s=REMAINDER
500 phrase$=" WHEN"
    & phrase$(4 TO LEN(phrase$))
510 END SELect
520 END DEFine the
530 :
540 DATA "NOW AND THEN"
550 DATA "IN DALE AND FEN"
560 DATA "FOX CREEPS FROM DEN"
570 DATA "MEN LOVE WOMEN"
580 DATA "WOMEN LOVE MEN"
590 DATA "PRIESTS CRY AMEN"
600 DATA "THE COLD BREEZE CHILLS"
610 DATA "THE SPARROW TRILLS"
620 DATA "THE BLACKBIRD SHRILLS"
630 DATA "THE BLOSSOM SPILLS"
640 DATA "SUN SHINES ON RILLS"
650 DATA "THE CHILL STREAMS FLOW"
660 DATA "THE WARM WINDS BLOW"
670 DATA "THE DAISIES GROW"
680 DATA "YOUTHS WILD OATS SOW"
690 DATA "WE THINK OF SNOW"
700 DATA "AS WE ALL KNOW"
710 DATA "BOTH HIGH AND LOW"
720 DATA "THE BRIGHT STARS GLOW"
730 DATA "THE SKYLARKS SING"
740 DATA "THE BLUEBELLS RING"
750 DATA "THE SWALLOWS WING"
760 DATA "IN GLORIOUS SPRING"
770 DATA "FORGET LIFE´S STING"
780 DATA "THE MAIDENS SING"
790 DATA "KIDS ROCK AND SWING"
800 DATA "JOY FILLS EACH THING"
```

Figure 4.2 (*continues*)

```
810  DATA "THIS WAY TIME FLIES"
820  DATA " 'NEATH BRIGHT BLUE SKIES"
830  DATA "BIRDS FILL THE SKIES"
840  DATA "LOVERS FORGE TIES"
850  DATA "THE OLD YEAR DIES"
860  DATA "KIDS COUNT MAGPIES"
870  DATA "AND LIFE TELLS LIES"
880  DATA "THE INSECTS CHATTER"
890  DATA "THE GOSSIPS NATTER"
900  DATA "THE RAINDROPS SPATTER"
910  DATA "THE CHILD'S FEET PATTER"
920  DATA "THE SEEDLINGS SCATTER"
930  DATA "THE BEASTS GROW FATTER"
940  DATA "WHAT DOES IT MATTER"
950  DATA "THE MAYFLIES DANCE"
960  DATA "THE PONIES PRANCE"
970  DATA "SHY LOVERS GLANCE"
980  DATA "MAYFLIES ENTRANCE"
990  DATA "TREES DON DISGUISE"
1000 DATA "LOVE FOOLS THE WISE"
1010 DATA "TEMPERATURES RISE"
1020 DATA "THE POETS RHYME"
1030 DATA "IN SUMMER TIME"
1040 DATA "CARILLONS CHIME"
1050 DATA "LOVE ACTS ITS MIME"
1060 DATA "WE WASH OFF GRIME"
1070 DATA "THE SUN MELTS RIME"
```

Figure 4.2

The basic rule of rhyme is that two syllables (not words) rhyme if they end with the same vowel and the same consonant sounds. So 'send' and 'end' rhyme because they have the same vowel and final consonant sounds. So do 'feed' and 'mead' even though they do not look the same, because (despite what you might have been taught at school) a vowel is not a unit of writing but a unit of sound, as is a consonant. They are not units of spelling, except in a secondary way. The computer can only recognize what are called 'sight rhymes', that is words which look the same whether they sound similar or not. Consequently we must construct our database of phrases so that all phrases that end the same in spelling will also sound the same, and we have to accept that phrases which sound the same but are spelled differently will not be paired by the program.

Both of these problems could be overcome with a certain amount of work. As well as representing our phrases as strings of characters we could also hold a dictionary of codes representing the sound pattern of the final syllables. There is actually a large number of such potential patterns, at least ($8 \times 35 \times 35$), so we would not attempt to encode them all, but we could employ quite an extensive coding system and hold the values in array elements which corresponded to the position of the phrases in the database. This would get over the problem. I leave it as an exercise for any interested reader and would be interested to see any results.

The problem of linking phrases coherently could be approached in a variety of ways. The best approach would be to hold a semantic representation of each phrase (as well as its written and aural representation) and choose links between phrases which fitted the semantics of both. For example, suppose we had the three phrases: 'Life is good', 'I wouldn't like to die' and 'I want to end it all'. The semantics of these phrases could include a flag which says whether the phrase is 'optimistic' or 'pessimistic'. If two successive phrases are flagged in the same way they could be joined by either the word 'so' or the word 'because', but if they are flagged as opposite to each other they would be joined by the word 'but' or the word 'though'. Consequently we would get complete sentences like 'I want to end it all but I don't want to die because life is good' or 'Life is good though I want to end it all but I don't want to die'.

However, to carry out such detailed semantic marking adequately would be a long job and would depend on the programmer's ability to identify all the possible kinds of semantic feature that a phrase might have. So Versificator treats its couplets as impressionistic lists of phrases. Sometimes they are related but sometimes they are just lists. If just a list, then a comma is placed between the two phrases: 'The buds are growing, the birds are singing, life is great.' However, if the phrase held in the database begins with 'the' the program may choose to replace it with 'as', 'like' or 'when'. All of these are relatively neutral conjunctions, except that they perhaps imply more of a causal connection between two events than a simple comma does. At any rate they add some variety to the verse and there are even some occasions where the same phrase occurring firstly with 'the' and then repeated with a conjunction actually sounds a little profound: 'The children play in the streets. Bombs are falling as children play in the streets.' Remember that earlier on we found that one simple form of creativity is creativity by repetition. Repetition with variation is one of the fundamental principles of all types of art.

If you find the idea of semantic marking for 'units' of poetry an interesting one you will find the concept expanded in a different context later in the book when we look at the semantic features of words and phrases in more detail.

4.4 Versificator—the program

The basis of this program (listed as Fig. 4.2), has just been described. As with previous programs we have a small database of phrases each of which can be half the line of a poem. These are combined into the actual rhyming couplets.

Firstly (line 120) a random number T determines how many couplets there are to be in the poem. The FOR . . . NEXT loop beginning at line 130 will be executed T times. Each time it cycles four phrases are chosen from the data. The first three times (controlled by the loop beginning at line 140) procedure choose is called and chosen phrase is printed.

Two tests operate within the loop, however. One (line 160) ensures that when the second phrase is chosen (i.e., the end phrase of the first line) the rhyming element of the phrase is stored in rhyme$ for future comparison and the phrase is stored in key$ to ensure that it is not chosen as a rhyme for itself in the next line. Procedure the is then called in order to determine the form of the connection between the first two phrases. The second test simply prints a blank line before the third phrase.

When these three phrases have been chosen and printed the fourth must be chosen but it is crucial that the chosen phrase should 'rhyme' with the second phrase yet should not be that phrase. Thus the choice of the phrase is continually repeated until the test in line 220 is true, i.e., the final syllable of the chosen phrase is equal to the syllable stored in rhyme$, and the chosen phrase is not the same as key$.

Procedure the is then called again to create the connection between phrases three and four, the phrase is printed and the routine loops round to print the next stanza if there is one.

Only three functions/procedures are needed to keep this main routine working. Firstly function syllable$ returns the final two letters in a chosen phrase. Rhyme is not always signalled by just the final two letters. Sometimes words may rhyme one or more syllables before the final syllable, sometimes words may end in the same two letters but not rhyme (e.g., talk and sulk). However, in the database we have used identity of the last two letters is a sufficient test for full rhyme.

If you wish to adapt the program to deal with more complex data, a more complete test would match the final vowel and the final consonant group. However, as the consonant groups of different words may vary between 0 and 5 and vowels may be 1 or 2 such a test needs to be more complex than that used here.

Procedure choose does what it says. It selects a random phrase from the data by generating a random number and restoring the data pointer to a given line dependent on that random number.

Procedure the is there to do a simple job but, as so often is the case with AI and text processing, the apparently simple may require most work. What is required is for the program to choose a possible connection between two given phrases. It is only called for the second and the fourth phrase. A random number s is chosen. If $s=1$ or the given phrase does not begin with 'THE', then the procedure goes no further and the phrase is printed exactly as it is in the data statement. However, if the phrase begins with 'THE' and s is not equal to 1, then the program can select a replacement for the 'THE'. The replacement is random and will be 'AS' or 'LIKE' or 'WHEN'. These are three possible conjunctives which do not carry much causal meaning, so it seldom matters what the preceding phrase is. In fact bisociating two arbitrary phrases like this with an apparent connection can force the reader to look for some connection between the two and regard the comparison as appropriate in some sense. Impressionistic poetry often uses such devices, relying on the intuition of the reader to provide individual connections.

4.5 Creating a story

Unfortunately designing a program to write a novel is well beyond the scope of this book. As we have already seen there are story-writing programs and they produce texts which are in some ways like human stories but in others very unlike them. They tend to be very repetitive, to be too literal, to relate trivial details and generally to be rather tedious and unoriginal. However, things are getting better and our understanding of the nature of story writing is gradually improving. Because it is a relatively new area and because little very successful work has been done it is one area where a gifted amateur stands a chance of doing some original work, so I am going to spend a short time describing what a story-writing program might do in the hope that someone will find the ideas sufficiently interesting to work on them. The desire to do so is not as odd as it might seem. Story telling is a fundamental part of normal human communication. In particular it forms a significant part of the processes of learning and retention. Many children find problems with story writing and with associated learning skills and self-expression.

Any program, no matter how intelligent, which would help such children write stories and to express themselves would be very welcome in primary schools around the country.

We can approach story writing from a large number of different viewpoints. This is one of the difficulties with modelling creativity of this complexity—different story tellers seem to proceed in different ways and many of them do not really know what they are doing when they create a story. An intelligent computer model, however, does not have to do exactly what a human being does, it only has to produce results which are like a human's. So what we would want of a computer story writer is a program which is general enough to produce many different stories which are like human stories, but need not match any particular human process. This means that any insights we have into story writing might lead to useful routines in a program.

If we look at the process of writing a story as a top-down process (i.e., something like a structured approach to writing a program—start with the broad design then gradually refine it) we might want our program to do each of the following in turn:

1. Select a genre—will the story be a thriller, a fantasy, science fiction, historical?
2. Select a main character. Usually called 'the protagonist' this will be the character who appears in most if not all the events in the story. She or he will have various attributes of personality, appearance, social standing, etc., and these may be relevant to the story, depending on the genre of story that has been selected. Thus, selecting the genre will set the flags to determine which of the character variables need values assigning to them.
3. Select a setting. This is the broad description of the environment in which the story will occur. Again it must be appropriate both to the genre and the character. Selection of genre, character and setting will define a vocabulary which it is appropriate to use in this kind of story. For example, if the genre is 'thriller' it will be inappropriate to use words like 'dragon's bane', 'cattle rustler', 'moon explorer' and so on.
4. Select a plot structure. There is undoubtedly a limit to the number of plots used in stories. The trouble is that no one has ever listed them in a way which is both satisfactory and useful. However, the program does not need a full choice of all possible plots and can be restricted to a few likely ones which fit the chosen genre. At this level of choice plot structures can be quite abstract like 'Protagonist loses something then finds it again' or 'Protagonist desires something so goes looking for it and eventually finds (or does not find) it'. The easiest way to create a list of these is to try to

summarize as broadly as possible the plots of stories which are classics in their genres, such as Gunfight at O.K. Corral, Star Wars, Lord of the Rings or Goldfinger.
5. Divide the plot into a series of episodes.
6. Write an introduction.
7. Write each episode.
8. When all episodes have been written, add a conclusion.

Each of these would of course be a subroutine or procedure. We can create a set of rewrite rules to describe the processes in each procedure just as we have for creating sentences. For example, we could say that an introduction could be described as follows:

Introduction = protag + setting + problem
protag = name (+ attribute)
name = {Fred, Prince Charming, Eloise}
attribute = at (+ attribute)
at = {handsome, wealthy, poor, brave}
setting = place (+ time)
place = {the palace, the market, home}
time = {early one morning, one midsummer's eve}
problem = po (+ problem)
po = {has no money, wants to get married, has lost his/her memory}

Just as we used the sentence grammar to generate English sentences so we can use this story grammar to generate the introduction to our story. One possible structure would be:

Prince Charming + the palace + early one morning + has lost his memory

Additional rules of the same kind would translate this structure into a proper sentence, such as: 'Early one morning Prince Charming awoke in the palace to find he had lost his memory.'

The key to a coherent story, however, is obviously the plot. As described above, a plot is a series of connected episodes and a complete plot could be regarded as a progam structure like the following:

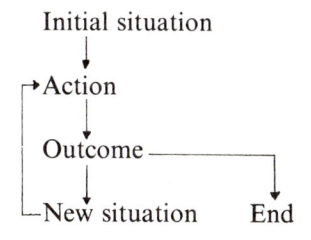

```
    Initial situation
           │
           ▼
  ┌─► Action
  │        │
  │        ▼
  │   Outcome ──────┐
  │        │        │
  │        ▼        ▼
  └── New situation  End
```

An episode would be an action which has an outcome, the outcome being either the end of the story or a new situation to which the protagonist responds with a new action. In this way the plot is advanced by the actions of its characters. Each event consists therefore of one or more actors, an action by the actor(s), the situation (time, place and circumstance) in which the action occurs and any objects or instruments used as part of that action, together with any actual or implied reasons for the action. Such reasons are usually related to the goal of the main character, which in turn depends on the overall purpose of the character as set out in the plot structure. Each episode must therefore be linked to the one following it by statements such as 'because', 'therefore' and 'then' as a way of showing the connections and the sequence between them.

A program to do this must therefore operate the following rules for each event:

1. Choose an actor in the current situation.
2. Select one of the goals of that character or a sub-goal within that goal.
3. Perform an action by that character in accord with the desired goal.
4. Write a connecting word or phrase.
5. Describe the resulting new situation.
6. If the plot structure has now been completed, then jump to the conclusion, otherwise go to Step 1.

(For our purposes a sub-goal is anything the character desires as a possible means of getting nearer to the main goal, established by the chosen plot structure. For example, in *Sleeping Beauty* the Prince's goal is to find the princess, but he has the sub-goals of cutting his way through the brambles and finding his way through the castle.)

You should be able to see that this kind of description is programmable in the same way that we set up sets of rules for sentences and verse. Using a description like this it is not too difficult to get programs which write stories like:

> One morning Steven found that he was poor. So he went into the town centre. Then he robbed an old lady. Then he was not poor any more. So he lived happily ever after.

But this is hardly a work of genius. To make such a story more interesting (and, of course, longer) more complex motivations are needed and the relationships between episodes and between characters must be much more complicated. Accidents can happen which are unrelated to main events. Characters can carry out actions whose sub-goals might not be revealed until very much later in the story. Different characters may have incompatible goals. There are a large number of complexities of this kind that need incorporating.

In addition, many stories are not structured in quite this linear way. Some have flash backs and flash forwards, or characters may pause and tell other stories, or a story within a story can begin, or two stories can be carried on side by side yet affecting each other. We must also consider the possibility of descriptive interludes (which amplify the descriptions of a single aspect of the current situation but may have no effect on the narrative structure).

And finally the rules for turning story structures into sentence structures are also many and varied. There is not a simple one-to-one correspondence between a narrative episode and a sentence. In some cases an episode may fill a whole chapter. In others it may be only part of a sentence.

I hope you can see that this is an interesting problem which, on the one hand, seems fundamentally simple (after all we know that all soap operas are the same, all fairy stories are the same, all murder mysteries are the same) and therefore easy to program, yet on the other hand has so many ramifications that it seems like one of those human facilities we will never satisfactorily be able to describe. I hope that some readers feel sufficiently interested by what is admittedly only a brief caricature of the problem to pursue their own story-writing programs.

5 Understanding natural language

5.1 General considerations

The key to making a micro act human is to make it understand language. Most human beings communicate with each other through language and it is the most natural means of communication available to us. Thus we would generally prefer it if we could get our meaning across in ordinary language to machines instead of having to understand the complexities of computer languages. As the aspect of computers which everyone sees and many people only ever encounter is input and output, it makes sense to try at least to get that input and output as close as possible to the language we normally use.

This is not as easy as it might sound. Language is a complex and varied phenomenon which is imperfectly understood. As with most other aspects of work in AI, most of the developments in language processing by machine have arisen from attempts to understand language further, and usually computer-based research on language does tell us something new about language but it also poses problems of greater and greater complexity. Some of these problems may be soluble with advances in hardware, but most are problems of software—we simply do not know enough about the way language works to build a perfect and complete model of language.

Some people even argue that there can be no such perfect and complete model. They argue that there is no such thing as 'language' in the abstract, only languages. And what they mean by languages is not what you and I might normally mean, such as French, English and Latin, but more specific varieties such as 'the language of schoolchildren', 'the language of computer scientists', 'the language of newspapers' and so on. Each language has its own context, a typical situation in which it is used, and in a different situation a different variety of language is used.

Thus there are two schools of thought in AI work on language. One attempts to establish models of language which depend on (or 'understand') a particular variety of language, while others try to establish grammars which can be used for any purpose and in any context, using rules for producing and understanding language that could apply to any variety of language in any situation. The latter are difficult and largely unsuccessful in practical terms. People have such a large range of language skills, use so many different linguistic rules and vary their language so remarkably that no model has come close to modelling the endless possible variety of real human language.

However, models of language within limited areas or limited context have had some success. This is because a particular variety of language used in a very limited context generally has a limited set of rules and a limited vocabulary. In this book it has not been necessary for me to write in blank verse, or to use the vocabulary of cookery or to write things like 'POLICE FOUND SAFE UNDER BLANKET' because poetry, cookery and newspapers are outside the current context. However, you will find words like 'RAM', 'micro' and 'keyboard' because these are part of the vocabulary of computer books, and you will similarly find phrases like 'If you examine the listing below you will see three variables' because this is the style of a book aiming to instruct. As the domain is limited it seems that it should be easier to specify all the rules for that particular variety, so that, providing you converse with the computer only in one particular variety, the computer will have the rules for keeping up its end of the conversation.

The analysis of language by computer is usually called 'parsing'. We will examine three different strategies for parsing. While not forgetting the need to consider context we will put it on one side for the moment.

5.2 A two-word parse

The simplest form of 'real English' input is the conventional two-word command of adventure games as in 'TAKE SWORD' or 'KILL DRAGON'. Slightly more elaborate versions allow several such commands to be strung together using 'AND', as in 'TAKE SWORD AND KILL DRAGON' and the use of prepositions such as 'WITH' as in 'TAKE SWORD AND KILL DRAGON WITH SWORD'.

Such parsers depend on a dictionary of allowed words. A typical routine which can cope with the NOUN + VERB structure and the words 'AND' and 'WITH' is given in Fig. 5.1. Its dictionary of allowed words is held in an array called dictionary$. I have not set up an actual dictionary here as this is only a routine to be incorporated in a larger program. The essential features of such a dictionary are that it should hold both the nouns and the verbs and that the variables noun_number and verb_number should hold the

```
10 REM Decode input commands
20 DEF PROCedure command
30 IF conj = 1 THEN
40 text$ = temp$
50 ELSE
60 putin
70 END IF
80 conj = 0
90 sp = " " INSTR text$
100 IF sp = 0 THEN
110 error
120 RETURN
130 END IF
140 vr$ = text$(1 TO sp-1)
150 text$ = text$(LEN(text$)-sp TO LEN(text$))
160 IF LEN(vr$)>5 THEN vr$ = vr$(1 TO 5)
170 word vr$,verb_number,verb_start
180 IF number = 0 THEN
190 error
210 RETURN
230 END IF
240 v% = number
250 sp = " " INSTR text$
260 IF sp<>0 THEN
270 n$ = text$(1 TO sp-1)
280 ELSE
290 n$ = text$
300 END IF
310 IF LEN(n$)>5 THEN n$ =n$(1 TO 5)
320 IF n$(LEN(n$)) = "S" THEN n$ = n$(1 TO LEN(n$)-1)
330 IF text$<>n$ THEN
340 text$ = text$ (LEN(text$)-sp TO LEN(text$))
350 ELSE
360 text$ = ""
370 END IF
```

Figure 5.1 (*continues*)

```
380 word n$,noun_number,noun_start
390 IF number = 0 THEN
400 error
420 RETURN
440 END IF
450 n1% = number
460 IF text$ = "" THEN RETURN
470 REPEAT loop
480 IF text$(1 TO 3) = "AND" THEN
490 conj = 1
500 E$ = "AND"
510 temp$ = text$(LEN(text$)-4 TO LEN(text$))
520 text$ = ""
530 EXIT loop
540 END IF
550 IF text$(1 TO 4) = "WITH" THEN
560 prep = 1
570 text$ = text$(LEN(text$)-5 TO LEN(text$))
580 END IF
590 sp = " " INSTR text$
600 IF sp<>0 THEN
610 n$ = text$(1 TO sp-1)
620 ELSE
630 n$ = text$
640 END IF
650 IF text$<>n$ THEN
660 text$ = text$(LEN(text$)-sp TO LEN(text$))
670 ELSE
680 text$ = ""
690 END IF
700 IF n$<>"" THEN  word n$,noun_number,noun_start
710 n2% = number
720 IF text$ = "" OR (sp = 0 AND number = 0) THEN EXIT loop
```

Figure 5.1 (*continues*)

```
730 END REPeat loop
740 END DEF command
750 :
760 REM Input routine
770 DEF PROCedure putin
780 REPEAT loop
790 PRINT
800 INPUT "WHAT NOW",text$
810 IF text$<>"" THEN EXIT loop
820 END REPeat loop
830 CLS
840 i = 0
850 REPEAT loop
860 i = i+1
870 l% = FNt(i)
880 IF l%>90 THEN text$(i) = CHR$(l%-32)
890 IF FNt(i)<65 AND FNt(i)<>32 THEN
900 text$ = FNl(i-1)+ FNr
910 i = i-1
920 END IF
930 IF FNt(i) = 32 AND FNt(i+1) = 32 THEN
940 text$ = FNl(i-1)+ FNr
950 i = i-1
960 END IF
970 IF i = LEN(text$) THEN EXIT loop
980 END REPeat loop
990 END DEF putin
1000 :
1010 REM Sundry text splitting functions
1020 DEF FNt(t) = ASC(text$(t))
1030 DEF FNr = text$(LEN(text$)-i TO LEN(text$))
1040 DEF FNl(l) = text$(l)
1050 :
1060 REM Inform player of errors
1070 DEF PROCedure error
1080 PRINT text$;" IS A MISTAKE"
1090 END DEF error
```

Figure 5.1 (*continues*)

```
1900 :
2000 DEF PROCedure
word(string$,total,start)
2010 number=0
2020 FOR i = start to start+total
2030 IF dictionary$(i)=string$ THEN
number=i
2040 NEXT i
2050 END DEF word
```

Figure 5.1

number of nouns and verbs respectively, while noun__start and verb__start hold the numbers of the array elements which hold the first noun and the first verb respectively.

Initially the routine tests to see if the conjunction flag (conj) is set, in line 30. If it is then the string held in temp$ is transferred to text$. If the flag is not set then the input procedure putin is called. Procedure putin requests a command and then carries out various editing functions upon the string. It changes all letters to capitals (line 880), removes all characters that are not letters or spaces (line 890) and deletes all superfluous spaces (line 940). This removes some possible errors and ensures that the text is in suitable form for comparison with the dictionary.

Whether the conjunction flag was set or not, by line 80 text$ has some text in it and it is this text that the rest of the routine parses. Firstly a check is made to ensure that there are at least two words. Line 90 looks for a space and if none is found the error routine is called. (We assume that if there is a space it is separating two words.)

The first word of text$ is now placed in vr$. This is assumed to be the verb because commands usually begin with verbs. The word is identified as all characters up to the first space (line 140). The word is also removed from text$. Line 160 assumes that all verbs are five characters or less. This ensures (a) that a player can type in just the first five letters of the verb and be sure that it will be detected, a useful feature with verbs like 'annihilate'; and (b), that different forms of the same verb can be classed together—for example the forms 'murder', 'murdering' and 'murdered' will all be regarded as the same. For some applications this is a drawback because we want the parser to be sensitive to different verb forms.

Procedure word is now called to establish if the verb is in the dictionary.

The procedure is also used by the noun finding parts of the routine, so it needs information about where in the dictionary to start looking, where to end and what it is looking for. These are the parameters which are passed to the routine. It is looking for vr$, starting at the first verb in the dictionary (verb__start) and continuing until it has looked at all the verbs (verb __number). Line 2030 does a simple comparison between the input string and the string held in the current element of the array, and if a match is found records the element number in a variable called number. Control is then returned to the calling routine.

Line 180 now checks to see that the verb was matched in the dictionary. If number is equal to zero, then no match was found, the error message is printed and the routine aborts. If number is not equal to zero, then its value is stored in the variable v% and this becomes a control variable in other routines in the program which respond to particular verbs.

We now repeat the procedure for the next word, but this time we are looking for a noun. As before, the next space is found, the word up to that space is stripped off and it is checked for length. One additional test is applied here in line 320. If the word ends in 'S', this is removed. This is in order to reduce plural words to a singular equivalent. Of course it also distorts words like 'GRASS' and there are plural forms which do not end in 'S', so for certain dictionaries this test may simply complicate matters.

As with the verb, procedure word is called to find the noun, but with n$, noun__start and noun__number as parameters. If no match is found, the error report is given and the routine aborts; otherwise the number of the noun is held in n1%.

A simple two-word parser would end here but ours goes on to analyse the remaining text if there is any. It repeatedly cycles through the text one word at a time. If it finds the word 'AND', then it sets the conjunction flag, moves the whole of the remaining text into temp$, wipes text$ clean and returns to the main routine. Once the main routine has acted upon the decoded input, then procedure command will again be called but now, of course, the conjunction flag is set so no input is requested and temp$ is sent into text$ instead.

If 'AND' is not found, then the routine looks for 'WITH'. If it finds it, the preposition flag prep is set, the word is removed and the routine looks for the next noun, which will be the noun that is being used in the 'with' part of the text, i.e., the prepositional phrase. The search for this second noun proceeds just as for the first, except that the resultant value, if found, is held in n2% instead of n1%. This means that, assuming a correctly formatted input text containing only words in the dictionary, the routine will end with values for v% and n1%, plus prep and n2% if the word 'WITH' is used. These are the values which will be used by the rest of the program to carry out decoding of the results and effects of the commands.

5.3 Getting words

Now we have seen how simple two-word commands can generally make sense in the context of adventure games. This is quite simply because the vocabulary of adventures is usually restricted to a list of nouns, representing the objects that can be manipulated in the program and a list of verbs representing the kinds of manipulation that can be carried out. There is only one grammatical rule and it cannot be varied: 'VERB + NOUN'. In normal English this rule is usually interpreted as a command, and playing the average adventure usually amounts to issuing a series of commands of the form 'TAKE x', 'MOVE y', 'EXTERMINATE z'.

But normal English is not restricted to commands. There are questions, statements, requests and so on. If you have played any adventures you will probably know the frustration of not being able to type in a complex command and being unable to think of a two-word way of saying the same thing. Even some commands cannot be expressed as two words. Consider 'Ask the dwarf to take the rock and drop it onto the dragon.' This does not seem like high Shakespearean verse, but it is too complex for most adventure programs. Thus we need to examine how we might make micro language processing more interesting and more useful. Although this chapter concentrates on input of language rather than on variety in output, there are several aspects of language processing which are common to both, and can therefore be used to improve the approaches discussed in the previous two chapters.

The first thing to do when analysing text is to get some input. Once we have it we must split it into words. You will remember that our simple adventure input divided input into two words by looking for a space and regarding everything before the space as the verb and everything after it as the noun. So one way to identify the words in a complete sentence is to mark the position of each space in a string and regard the items between spaces as complete words. This is good enough providing there is no punctuation and no extra spaces and the input ends with a space. Our routine must handle these problems. There would be two ways of doing this. One would be to take in the whole sentence using INPUT, then remove any superfluous spaces and unwanted punctuation. But perhaps a better approach is to write your own input routine which takes in one character at a time using INKEY$. If the character is a space and the previous character is a space, then it is to be ignored. If the character is punctuation, then it is to be ignored. If it is the ⟨Enter⟩ character, then the routine is ended, otherwise the character is stored in a string variable or array.

As in Sinclair SuperBASIC a string variable is equivalent to a one-dimensional string array there is really no difference in these two manners of storage. If we assume that no word will be longer than twelve characters and no input string longer than six words, we can dimension an array of six by twelve and we can get rid of all spaces and just use successive array elements for successive words.

Lines 150 and 350 in Fig. 5.12 illustrate a routine which replaces the standard INPUT routine. It acts like the standard INPUT command gathering a string of individual characters one character at a time until the ⟨Enter⟩ key is pressed. It has three differences from INPUT, however. Firstly it only accepts allowed characters, i.e., the letters A to Z and the space. If INPUT were used an error check would have to be carried out after the complete string had been typed in and, if disallowed characters had been entered, an error message would have to be printed and the message retyped. Using this routine to replace INPUT therefore saves time and makes the text processing more friendly for the user. It is important, however, that the user knows that only certain characters are allowed, so this must be stated in the instructions, otherwise many users will begin to think there is something wrong with their typing or their keyboard.

The second difference is that we are storing the input in the cells of an array, not in a single string. In Sinclair SuperBASIC this does not actually make much difference as substrings of strings can be addressed in a similar way to cells within arrays. Users of other BASICs will find, however, that this removes the need to use MID$ and related functions to cut up strings. However, we would not know where the spaces were in such a continuous string and would have to search for them. This routine removes that problem by dividing input as it is typed in into words and storing each word in a separate cell. Finally, and most important, is the fact that this routine can be altered. As we develop our input-processing algorithm we will see that other important tests need to be made as text is typed in, to save time later on.

The first of these tests, already mentioned, is to delete superfluous spaces. This test therefore says:

If current character is a space and last character is a space then ignore current character

This is carried out at line 290. The complete program is explained in Sec. 5.5.

5.4 Augmented transition network grammars

Quite a mouthful, isn't it? However, ATN grammars, as they are usually referred to, are not that complicated. In fact we have already looked at two rather simple examples. The 'two-word' parser above is one, and the sentence-generating program in Chapter 4 is another. The advantage of using a grammar as the basis for text routines in a computer program is that the same model, providing it is accurate enough, can be used both for production tasks and for parsing. In other words, if our grammar is efficient we can use the same model of language, maybe even the same routines, for both understanding input and for creating varied output.

If you think about it for a moment you will see that this makes sense. A grammar is meant to be an accurate description of human language. Human beings do not use one language for sending messages and another for receiving them, so the same grammar should fit both aspects of human talk. If it does this for human beings, there is no reason why it should not be able to do it for computers.

ATN grammars are not the most powerful of grammars used by linguists, but they have been some of the most successful in AI programming and in practical applications which use natural language. This is in part because they are easy to understand and easy to implement. Furthermore, once the principles are understood it is relatively easy to keep on adding to and modifying a given grammar to make something that is more satisfactory for a given purpose. One final reason is that ATN grammars correspond quite closely to certain approaches to programming, as we saw in the sentence generator.

The principle behind an ATN grammar is that a sentence during parsing is regarded as a series of states. It is parsed or generated from left to right with each state allowing a number of possible options or transitions. For example, our 'two-word' parser could be represented as in Fig. 5.2. This shows a series

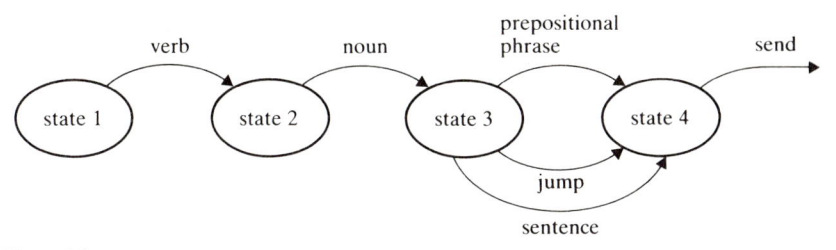

Figure 5.2

of four states. Passing between any two states can only be by successfully traversing one of the loops that leaves a state, otherwise an error is produced. From the first state only a verb provides a legal transition to the second state. From the second to the third only a noun provides a legal transition. We have three choices from state three to four however. One is just to jump to it, without finding anything. A second is to find a prepositional phrase. A third is to find a sentence. These correspond to the possibilities in the program of 'No further words', 'finding WITH' and 'finding AND'.

There is a distinction to be made between finding a noun or a verb and finding a sentence or a prepositional phrase, however. In the first case we are looking for words in a particular category. In other words we are carrying out the dictionary look-up procedure. But in the second case we are looking for structures, not word types. Such structures may themselves have a number of states. Obviously the search for another sentence within the sentence is a recursive procedure using the same series of states. A prepositional phrase could be described as in the structure in Fig. 5.3, made up of three states with three transitions. Find the word 'WITH', find a noun and send control back to the seeking routine.

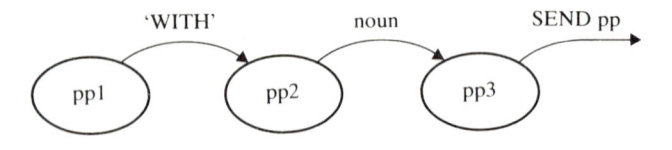

Figure 5.3

Thus there are several kinds of transition. One is to find a word in a particular category. A second is to find an exact word, such as 'WITH'. A third is to seek another structure by calling a subroutine, a fourth is to send control back to a calling routine and a fifth is simply to jump to the next state without doing anything.

Where there are several possible transitions from one state to the next the tests must be prioritized so that the most likely one is tried first. In our two-word program we tested first to see if there were any more words. If not we jumped straight to the end. We then tested for 'AND' and, if it was found placed the text to one side so that a search for another sentence could be made next time round. Finally we looked for 'WITH'. This gives us a priority of 1. JUMP, 2. SENTENCE and 3. PREP PHRASE. If we add these priorities plus information on the transition types to the original figure, we now have a reasonably complete ATN like Fig. 5.4.

This is fine as far as it goes but the grammar in this diagram is not a very complete model of English. It is basically correct but it needs a fair number of additions.

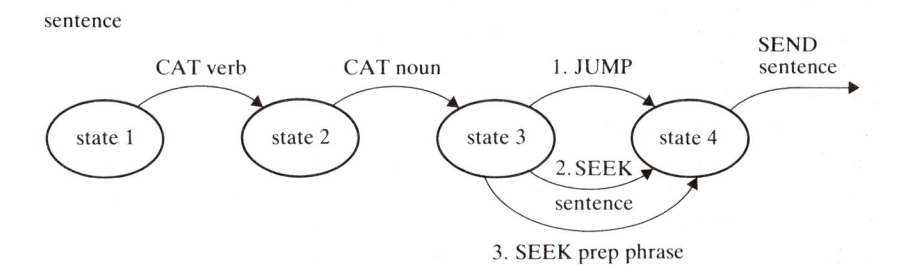

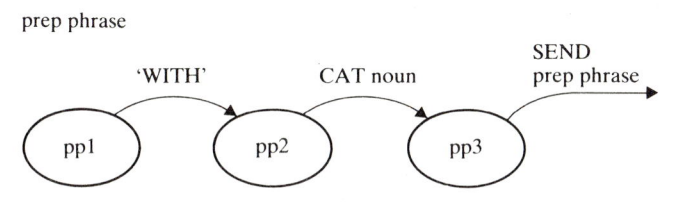

Figure 5.4

In the first place not all sentences are commands. In fact the most common sentence structure is that which we found in the sentence generator—a noun phrase followed by a verb phrase. So we have two choices of transition from the first state. We can look for a noun phrase or we can look for a verb. As most commands request actions they usually begin with action verbs, so we can make the parse more exact by specifying that the verb must be an action verb. This means, of course, that not only do we have to mark dictionary items with their word class but also any subclasses within that main class. For example, before we are finished we will want not only action verbs but also auxiliary verbs.

We will want auxiliaries because some sentences are questions. A common form of question begins with an auxiliary verb, such as 'Do you hate the Commodore 64?' This gives us three possible transitions from state 1—noun phrase, action verb or auxiliary verb. These correspond roughly to the sentence types 'statement', 'command' and 'question'. (This correspondence is something we will explore further when we examine speech acts later in the book.)

Both auxiliaries and action verbs are types of words so the relevant information can be held in the dictionary, but a noun phrase is a structure so this transition will have to be a seeking loop which tries to find the substructure at the beginning of a sentence. We must also decide which to test for first in order to assign priorities. In a real application such a decision depends a little on trial and error, as the designers discover the most common types of input that the particular system is likely to encounter. We have two conflicting guidelines to aid us. One says 'Put the most frequently encountered structure at priority 1 because this will save processing time.' The second says 'Put category tests at higher priority because they are easier to test for.' Let us assume that commands are the most common kind of input, questions the next most common and statements the least. This gives us Fig. 5.5.

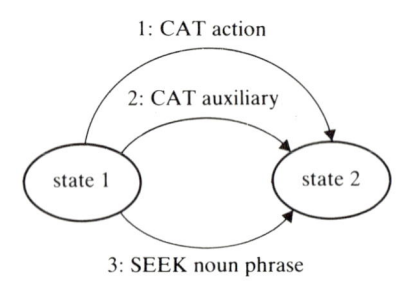

1: CAT action
2: CAT auxiliary
state 1
state 2
3: SEEK noun phrase

Figure 5.5

For the moment we will not worry about the structure of a noun phrase. Just remember that we have to come back to it. So, what comes next? Immediately we have a problem. The state following a successful test for an auxiliary verb is unlikely to be the state which follows a successful test for an action verb, which is different again from successfully finding a noun phrase. Consider the typical sentences 'Open the door', 'Is the door open?' and 'The door opens'. In the first and second examples the next unit is a noun phrase (just like our initial two-word parser) but in the third it is a verb. So we actually seem to require two possible states after the first successful test. If we pursue the analysis further we will see that after the noun phrase in example 1 we have nothing, but in example 2 we have a verb and a noun phrase. This

UNDERSTANDING NATURAL LANGUAGE 71

implies that we actually need three other states, and these would lead their own separate ways, as in Fig. 5.6.

This diagram shows the redundancy in the system. Effectively states 5, 7 and 8 are the same, as each of them can lead only to sending the completed sentence back to the calling routine. Also the pattern from state 3 to state 8 seems to be the same as that from state 1 through state 4 to state 7. So perhaps we could combine these and replace the state 1 to state 4 transition with a straightforward JUMP from state 1 to state 3. As we made 'SEEK noun phrase' the third priority, this would happen only if neither an auxiliary nor an action verb were found first, so it seems plausible. This gives us a more elegant grammar, as in Fig. 5.7.

We would want to add to this the possibility that prepositional phrases could be tagged on at the end, to give input like 'Open the door with the key' or 'Is the book lying on the table', and we might also want adverbs to qualify the whole thing, as in 'Is the dog barking loudly?' or 'The man eats his soup noisily'. We can have sentences which have one, both or neither of these additions, and they can be added several times allowing sentences ranging

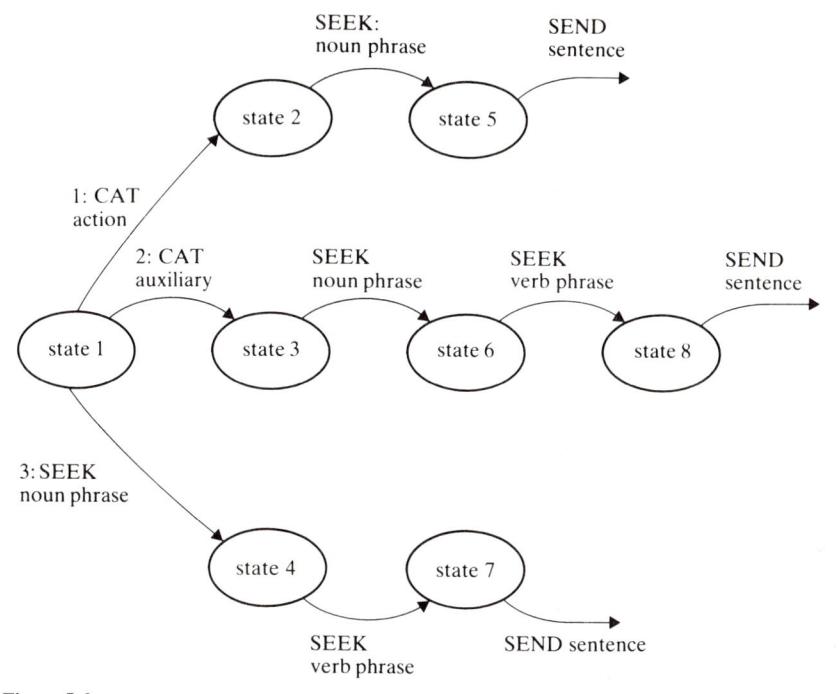

Figure 5.6

72 THE INTELLIGENT MICRO

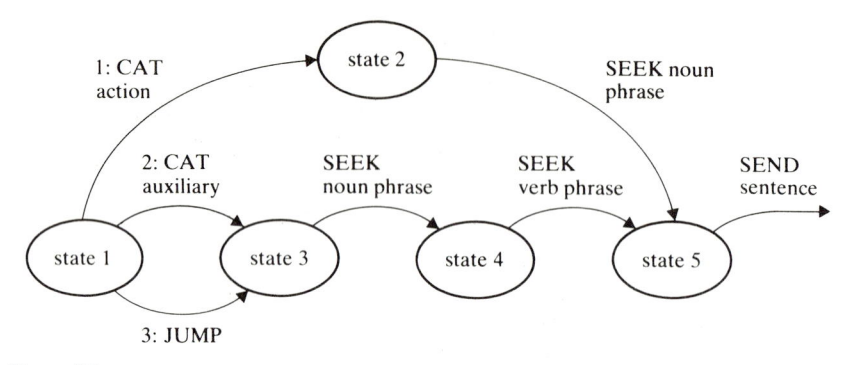

Figure 5.7

[Diagram: state 1 → (1: CAT action) → state 2 → (SEEK noun phrase) → state 5 → SEND sentence; state 1 → (2: CAT auxiliary) → state 3 → (SEEK noun phrase) → state 4 → (SEEK verb phrase) → state 5; state 1 → (3: JUMP) → state 3]

from 'The dog barks' to 'The dog barks noisily at the cat in the shed' to 'Did Jim write the letter about the computer yesterday with his pen?' To do this we simply add two loops to the final state called 'SEEK prepositional phrase' and 'CAT adverb'. Then, while there remain words to be parsed, the program can perpetually test both loops in turn.

This gives us a complete ATN grammar at the level of the sentence as in Fig. 5.8. However it is not complete because the structures Noun Phrase, Verb Phrase and Prepositional Phrase are undefined. There is no need to explore these in detail as the defining procedure remains the same. Figure 5.9 summarizes a simple ATN description of a noun phrase, Fig. 5.10 a verb phrase and Fig. 5.11 a prepositional phrase.

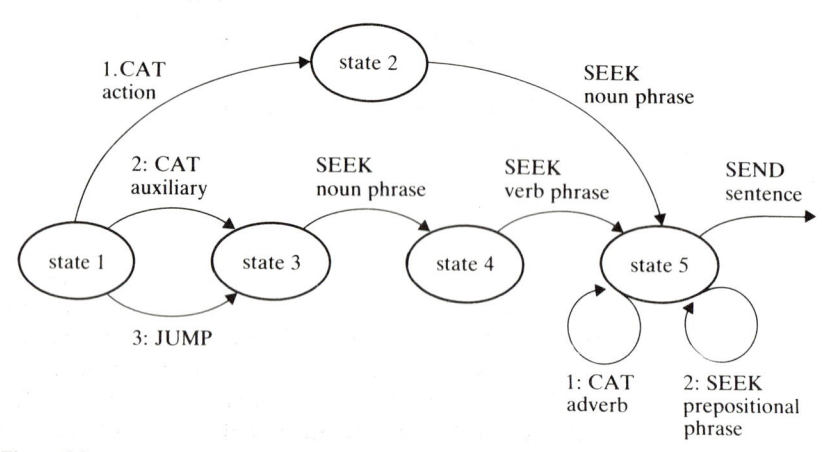

[Diagram: state 1 → (1. CAT action) → state 2 → (SEEK noun phrase) → state 5 → SEND sentence; state 1 → (2: CAT auxiliary) → state 3 → (SEEK noun phrase) → state 4 → (SEEK verb phrase) → state 5; state 1 → (3: JUMP) → state 3; state 5 has loops: 1: CAT adverb, 2: SEEK prepositional phrase]

Figure 5.8

UNDERSTANDING NATURAL LANGUAGE 73

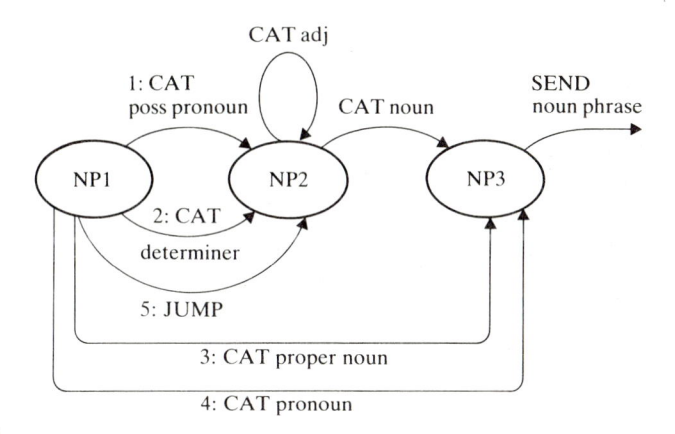

Figure 5.9

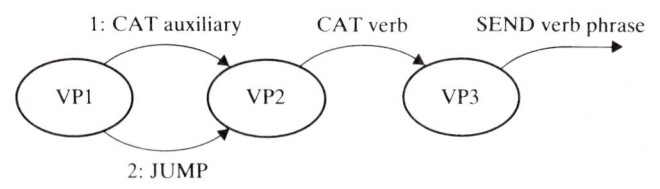

Figure 5.10

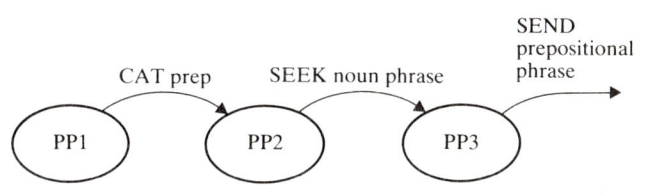

Figure 5.11

The noun phrase description permits such structures as 'his green book', 'Jim', 'the big white ship', 'people', 'we' and 'London'. The verb phrase permits only very simple structures containing verbs and possibly auxiliaries, like 'hits', 'is wishing', 'could lose'. Note that this means sentences with two auxiliary verbs are possible, as in 'Will Charles have had a nice day?' or 'Has the duck been taken to the vet's?'. The prepositional phrase allows only simple structures of preposition plus noun phrase. Note that this means that the noun phrase can be found at two different levels in the structure. In fact some English sentences (not allowed in this grammar) allow noun phrases to include prepositional phrases and prepositional phrases to include noun phrases, a recursive structure which could cause programming problems if pursued to any depth.

This gives a reasonable ATN grammar which can be used either to produce or to parse a wide range of sentences. Of necessity it is still rather simple and there are many types of grammatical sentence it would regard as ungrammatical, plus some ungrammatical ones it will accept. However, it is more comprehensive than can be currently found in any commercial games and most business software. Here is a list of improvements you might like to consider:

1. Add negatives (e.g., 'I do not want a QL').
2. Allow prepositional phrases at the beginning of a sentence (e.g., 'With his mighty sword Ardavarak slew the dragon').
3. Introduce relative clauses, i.e., clauses that begin with 'which', 'who' or 'that' (e.g., 'The programmer who wrote this is dyslexic').
4. Allow questions beginning with the so-called 'wh-words', i.e., 'who', 'what', 'where', 'when', 'why' and 'how' (e.g., 'Who is the king of Siam?').
5. Allow different conjunctions, such as 'and', 'but', 'because'. There are some problems with these little words as can be illustrated by the sentences 'The boy laughed and the girl sang' and 'The boy and the girl laughed and sang'.

5.5 The ATN program

As we have already observed in Chapter 4 a good grammar and a well-structured program to produce or analyse language are very much the same. Both are formal languages representing structures present in a less formal language. The ATN program in Fig. 5.12 looks in many ways like the diagrams of ATN grammar we have already examined. It is particularly easy in programs of this kind to code a formal grammar. In essence it is simply a question of taking each component of the grammar and writing an appropriate function or routine to carry out that component.

So in this program we have procedures which look for noun phrases, for verb phrases and for prepositional phrases, we have chunks of program which represent the main states that the grammar can pass through (called st1, st2, st3 and st5), we have tests at various points to see if the parse has failed at that point, and we have a chunk of program designed to test if a word is of a particular syntactic category.

```
110 RESTORE
120 CLS
130 CLEAR
140 init
150 letter$=""
160 t$="ABCDEFGHIJKLMNOPQRSTUVWXYZ " & CHR$(10)
170 w=8:l=12
180 DIM sentence$(w,l)
190 s=1
200 PRINT "Please type a sentence"
210 REPeat store
220 word$=""
230 REPeat wd
240 REPeat keyboard
250 letter$=INKEY$(0):IF letter$="" THEN GO TO 250
260 PRINT letter$;
270 IF letter$ INSTR t$ <>0 THEN EXIT keyboard
280 END REPeat keyboard
290 IF letter$ <> " " AND letter$ <> CHR$(13) THEN word$ = word$ & letter$
300 IF letter$=" " OR  letter$=CHR$(10) THEN EXIT wd
310 END REPeat wd
320 IF letter$=CHR$(10) THEN word$=word$(1 TO LEN(word$)-1)
330 sentence$(s)=word$
340 s=s+1
350 IF s=w OR letter$=CHR$(10) THEN EXIT store
360 END REPeat store
370 fail=0
380 cur_word=1
390 stl
400 IF fail=1 THEN PRINT "The parse has failed"
```

Figure 5.12 (*continues*)

```
410 STOP
420 :
430 DEFine PROCedure st1
440 PRINT "At st1"
450 IF cat(cur_word)=action THEN
460 PRINT sentence$(cur_word);" is an action verb"
470 cur_word=cur_word+1
480 st2
490 ELSE
500 IF cat(cur_word)=aux THEN
510 cur_word=cur_word+1
520 PRINT sentence$(cur_word);" is an auxiliary verb"
530 END IF
540 st3
550 END IF
560 IF fail=1 THEN RETurn
570 st5
580 IF fail=1 THEN RETurn
590 PRINT "A successful parse"
600 END DEFine st1
610 :
620 DEFine PROCedure st2
630 PRINT "At st2"
640 np
650 END DEFine st2
660 :
670 DEFine PROCedure st3
680 PRINT "At st3"
690 np
700 IF fail=1 THEN RETurn
710 vp
720 END DEFine st3
730 :
740 DEFine PROCedure st5
750 PRINT "At st5"
760 REPeat stloop
```

Figure 5.12 (*continues*)

```
770 IF sentence$(cur_word)="" OR fail=1
THEN EXIT stloop
780 IF cat(cur_word)=adverb THEN
790 cur_word=cur_word+1
800 ELSE
810 pp
820 END IF
830 END REPeat stloop
840 END DEFine st5
850 :
860 DEFine PROCedure np
870 PRINT "Seeking noun phrase"
880 IF cat(cur_word)=proper THEN
890 PRINT sentence$(cur_word);" is a proper noun"
900 cur_word=cur_word+1
910 RETurn
920 END IF
930 IF cat(cur_word)=pronoun THEN
940 PRINT sentence$(cur_word);" is a pronoun"
950 cur_word=cur_word+1
960 RETurn
970 END IF
980 IF cat(cur_word)=poss THEN
990 PRINT sentence$(cur_word);" is a possessive pronoun"
1000 cur_word=cur_word+1
1010 END IF
1020 IF cat(cur_word)=det THEN
1030 PRINT sentence$(cur_word);" is a determiner"
1040 cur_word=cur_word+1
1050 END IF
1060 REPeat adjloop
1070 IF cat(cur_word)=adj THEN
1080 PRINT sentence$(cur_word);" is an adjective"
```

Figure 5.12 (*continues*)

```
1090 cur_word=cur_word+1
1100 ELSE
1110 EXIT adjloop
1120 END IF
1130 END REPeat adjloop
1140 IF cat(cur_word)<>noun THEN fail=1:RETurn
1150 PRINT sentence$(cur_word);" is a noun"
1160 cur_word=cur_word+1
1170 END DEFine np
1180 :
1190 DEFine FuNction cat(cur_word)
1200 LOCal a
1210 a=0
1220 i=1
1230 PRINT "Considering :";sentence$(cur_word)
1240 REPeat loop
1250 IF sentence$(cur_word)= dictionary$(i) THEN
1260 a=i
1270 EXIT loop
1280 END IF
1290 IF i=word_no THEN EXIT loop
1300 i=i+1
1310 END REPeat loop
1320 IF a>0 THEN a=syntax%(a)
1330 RETurn a
1340 END DEFine cat
1350 :
1360 DEFine PROCedure pp
1370 PRINT "Seeking prepositional phrase"
1380 IF cat(cur_word)<> prep THEN fail=1:RETurn
1390 PRINT sentence$(cur_word);" is a preposition"
1400 temp_word=cur_word
1410 cur_word=cur_word+1
```

Figure 5.12 (*continues*)

```
1420 np
1430 IF fail=1 THEN cur_word=temp_word
1440 END DEFine pp
1450 :
1460 DEFine PROCedure vp
1470 PRINT "Seeking verb phrase"
1480 IF cat(cur_word)=neg THEN cur_word=cur_word+1
1490 IF cat(cur_word)<>verb THEN fail=1:RETurn
1500 PRINT sentence$(cur_word);" is a verb"
1510 cur_word=cur_word+1
1520 END DEFine vp
1530 :
1540 DEFine PROCedure init
1550 word_no=50
1560 DIM dictionary$(word_no,12)
1570 DIM syntax%(word_no)
1580 FOR i= 1 TO word_no
1590 READ dictionary$(i),syntax%(i)
1600 NEXT i
1610 cur_word=0
1620 true=1:false=0
1630 det=3
1640 noun=4
1650 adj=1
1660 adverb=2
1670 prep=5
1680 pronoun=6
1690 proper=7
1700 verb=9
1710 action=11
1720 poss=8
1730 aux=12
1740 neg=13
1750 END DEFine init
1760 :
1770 REMark Data
```

Figure 5.12 (*continues*)

```
1780 DATA "a",3
1790 DATA "the",3
1800 DATA "man",4
1810 DATA "lass",4
1820 DATA "big",1
1830 DATA "small",1
1840 DATA "yesterday",2
1850 DATA "again",2
1860 DATA "sometimes",2
1870 DATA "to",5
1880 DATA "by",5
1890 DATA "with",5
1900 DATA "you",6
1910 DATA "we",6
1920 DATA "me",6
1930 DATA "Fred",7
1940 DATA "Jim",7
1950 DATA "Sue",7
1960 DATA "Anne",7
1970 DATA "went",9
1980 DATA "goes",9
1990 DATA "liked",9
2000 DATA "saw",9
2010 DATA "come",11
2020 DATA "go",11
2030 DATA "bring",11
2040 DATA "take",11
2050 DATA "was",12
2060 DATA "does",12
2070 DATA "is",12
2080 DATA "did",12
2090 DATA "were",12
2100 DATA "not",13
2110 DATA "their",8
2120 DATA "my",8
2130 DATA "his",8
2140 DATA "her",8
2150 DATA "book",4
```

Figure 5.12 (*continues*)

```
2160 DATA "red",1
2170 DATA "blue",1
2180 DATA "green",1
2190 DATA "old",1
2200 DATA "young",1
2210 DATA "box",4
2220 DATA "chair",4
2230 DATA "computer",4
2240 DATA "house",4
2250 DATA "table",4
2260 DATA "dog",4
2270 DATA "cat",4
```

Figure 5.12 The ATN Program

As an ATN grammar really does only two things it is relatively easy to understand the program. All it is doing is checking that the syntactic category of each word in the sentence is allowed at that position in one (or more) of the possible structures, and that all the substructures fit together in an allowed manner. A grammar of this kind is actually no more than a series of rules which specify what is 'possible' or 'legal'. We can therefore talk about 'grammars of narrative', 'grammars of human behaviour', 'grammars of game playing' and so on, because these are rules which establish the components and the structures of a particular rule-governed activity.

Procedure init creates the dictionary. The variable word_no holds the number of words in the dictionary. It is convenient to use a variable for this rather than build the actual size of the dictionary into the program because such programs habitually change their databases as they are developed. If, for example, you wish to add more words to the dictionary, you need only change the declaration in line 1550 to the new total and do not need to worry about searching through the entire program to discover all the instances where a routine is controlled by the size of the dictionary.

The built-in dictionary has only 50 words divided into 12 syntactic categories. These categories are coded by the numbers 1 to 13, omitting 10 because of the confusion that 1 and I, O and 0 sometimes cause in hard copy. Lines 1630 to 1740 assign each of these values to a variable. Again this is for convenience rather than necessity. It ensures that each time we want to test, for example, for a verb we can write IF cat(cur_word) = verb THEN ... rather than IF cat(cur_word) = 9 THEN .... This makes each test easier to understand and more like the grammar it encodes. In addition the list between lines 1630 and 1740 can be used as an index to the word types held by the program if you are adding new words to the dictionary or expanding the testing procedures.

The dictionary itself is held in dictionary$. The code for the part of speech each word represents is held in a separate array, syntax%. I suggest that if you add other features to your grammar you hold each one in a separate array (if you are not worried by the amount of RAM your program needs) because the names of the arrays can once more provide clues to the nature of each procedure that reads from or writes to them. So, for example, if you added the notion of 'tense' to this grammar you might store the tense codes in an array called 'tense'.

Reading through the data statements shows another problem that is encountered in syntactic analysis. Although no word is actually used twice in the dictionary to make the grammar work correctly words like 'go' and 'bring' would have to be included twice, once as action verbs and once as verbs in their own right. Some main verbs can also be auxiliary verbs. Some prepositions can also be adverbs. Some nouns have the same form as some verbs. In all these cases a separate entry is needed, not only for each word form but also for each of the syntactic roles it might take. To overcome this while retaining the same basic approach it would be necessary to place multiple entries against each word form so that, for example, 'go' has the values 9 and 11 next to it to show that it can be both main verb and action verb. However, this means that the records for each word may be of different lengths, which involves irregular storage or wasted space and either way complicates the programming for a demonstration program.

Another init has set up the dictionary the main program then requests and receives a sentence from the user. The input routine is custom made to assign words to an array called sentence$ as they are typed in. In this program this saves very little time, but for long input strings it ensures that no time is wasted splitting up a string after the whole thing has been typed in. However, it is somewhat crude and does not, for example, permit deletion of errors, so type with extra care.

Once the sentence has been stored the control variables 'fail' and 'cur__word' are set. If at any point in the program fail is set to 1, then the parse has failed. Cur__word simply holds the number of the current word being examined. In a more complex ATN parse this variable would be increased as the depth of the search for structures increased and decreased as failure caused the searches of those structures to back up. However, there is no decrementing of cur__word in our program as it is only incremented following a success.

Control is then passed to the first state of the grammar, stl. If you have understood the grammar above, the rest of the program will be easily comprehended. It consists of structures which exactly replicate those in our symbolic grammar. So procedure stl tests first to see if the first word is an action verb. If it is, then control is passed to state2 (procedure st2); if not, then the program tests for an auxiliary verb. If an auxiliary is found, then cur__word is incremented to the next word. Whether an auxiliary is found or not control will then be passed to state three. If either st2 (in the case of an action verb) or st3 (in the case of an auxiliary) fail, then stl will end at line 560. If not, then control is passed to the final state, st5. This therefore encodes the flow of control represented by Fig. 5.8.

The other procedures simply represent the 'calls' made by the transitions in Fig. 5.8. Thus 'SEEK noun phrase' is a call to procedure np and 'SEEK verb phrase' a call to procedure vp. None of this should now seem complex. The only difficulties may appear when we decide where to put the 'increment cur__word' statements. For example, do we put one at the end of the noun phrase routine (to be carried out when it has succeeded) or at the point at which control returns from such a routine to the calling procedure? Usually one would put such 'advance the pointer to next entry' statements within calling routines, as we can be certain that it will only be carried out at the right moment, while the called routine might be called at any number of places. The deeper the search the more likely we are to become confused by the way the pointer is advanced (or moved back).

A second problem that has to be overcome concerns the loops that, in principle, could continue indefinitely, such as the 'CAT adverb' loop and the 'SEEK prepositional phrase' loop in Fig. 5.8. We have to ensure that either or both can be executed in any order in order to encode the grammar exactly. So, for example, if the end of a sentence was 'adverb + pp + adverb + adverb' our routine has to accept this, as well as 'pp + pp + adverb + pp' and 'adverb + pp + pp + adverb' and any other combinations you care to think of. In such cases we will probably have to write different sets of code for different situations. But for this particular example we have three choices: (1) if there are no more words, then we have successfully parsed the thing so can end the routine; (2) the next word could be an adverb; (3) the next word may be part of a prepositional phrase. We would have a problem if a prepositional phrase could begin with an adverb (because then how would we know if a particular adverb stands on its own or as part of a prepositional phrase?) but our grammar does not allow such a construction.

We can cope with this by giving tests in two stages. Firstly we establish if there are any more words. If not, then we have condition (1) (line 770). If there are, we test for an adverb. If this test fails we test for a prepositional phrase, but if it succeeds then the pointer cur__word is advanced and we go back to the 'end of the sentence?' test. If the prepositional phrase test succeeds, this also causes the pointer to be advanced and the routine cycles to line 770 as for an adverb. If it fails, then the flag fail is set to 1 and line 770 ends the routine. If we had three such loops instead of two, then we would need embedded IF ... THEN ... statements between lines 780 and 830.

Output from the program is not spectacular. It simply reports on its progress (which part of the ATN it has currently reached, which state it has achieved), tells the user which words it is looking at and reports when it finds a word of the right type in what it regards as the right place. However, it can correctly parse quite complex sentences, ranging from 'Take the old red book to the man with the young blue dog again' to 'Did Fred like the old red book by the blue computer?' The range of acceptable sentences can become quite large with a suitably extended vocabulary.

However, such a program is of little use on its own (unless you are a lecturer in languages). The best way to adapt it for practical purposes is to rewrite each of the statements which say sentence$(cur__word);" is a xxx" (e.g., line 460). Replace each of these lines with a line which stores the appropriate syntactic code in another array (call it parse). This coding of the sentence is its syntactic pattern and can become the basis of decoding routines. For example, a likely use for such a routine would be in a database query system, in which case it would be important to know whether the user was giving a command to the system, adding a statement to the database or querying the data. Looking at the syntax code in parse(1) will tell you this. If it is 11, then the sentence is a command. If it is 12 it is a question. If it was something else, then it is a statement. So use the SELect ON ... in SuperBASIC or ON ... GOSUB ... in other BASICs statement to send control appropriately to the executing procedures. For example,

```
3000 REM Controlling action according to an
input sentence
3010 var = parse(1)
3020 SELect ON var
3030  = 11 : command
3040  = 12 : query
3050  = REMAINDER : statement
3060 END SELect
```

In a similar way the decisions within these major routines can test appropriate parts of the parsed sentence. For example, suppose that the input sentence was 'Did Jim see Sue?' (we are assuming a modified dictionary)

and suppose the program has 'understood' that the sentence is a question because it begins with the auxiliary verb 'did'. It now needs to know what the main verb is so it looks through array parse until it finds code 9. This will be in parse(3) because the verb is the third word in the sentence. It can then try to identify who did the seeing, and who or what was seen, by looking for two noun phrases. The 'seer' is the noun phrase before the main verb and the 'seen' is the noun phrase after it. The program now 'understands' the question and can attempt to answer it by examining its data to see if any information relating to Jim or Sue is held within it.

In fact grammars have been constructed which act in this way. They have proved most useful in natural language query systems for databases but are not generally 'pure' ATN grammars. They use information about the concepts underlying words like 'see' of the kind we have just illustrated in an attempt to discover patterns in input which are not purely syntactic. However, as this is really a different subject we will return to it when we look at pattern recognition.

6 Pattern matching

6.1 Introduction

A problem common to several areas of artificial intelligence research is that of pattern recognition and matching. It applies most importantly in the realm of perception, though, as we shall see, many realms of human information processing have their own patterns, so the problems are pervasive. Perception has two aspects. Firstly there is the process by which external stimuli are actually received by an organism or machine. Eyes or cameras provide the receptors for light impulses. Microphones or ears provide receptors for sound. Other mechanisms can detect other forms of energy and changes of energy. As you will probably know the chemical, electrical and mechanical processes involved in receiving such signals are well understood and artificial sensors can in many respects exceed the performance of our human equivalents.

But this is only half the story. Once signals have been received they have to be processed to extract some form of message, i.e., the signals have to be made sense of. We do not really see objects. We see patterns of lines, angles, light, shadow, texture and shapes. The brain has to sort this chaos of signals into a coherent order. It has to decide, for example, if a small patch of grey of a different shade from the grey surrounding it is a small object nearby or a large object far away; if it is part of something else or a separate object; if it is a shadow cast by another object or if it is a solid mass. Such decisions are not made just on the basis of combinations of cues and clues in the patterns received but also on memories of previous situations, on information sent from other sensors and also on ideas we have about the world. For example, whether we see an object as 'a green dress' or 'a blue dress' is as much a function of the language we speak as the electromagnetic spectrum. Before the twelfth century nobody could 'see' orange objects because the concept of orange did not exist. The nearest a mediaeval peasant could come would be to talk of 'yellowy red' or 'reddy yellow' which you will probably agree do not mean the same thing as 'orange'.

It is difficult to analyse the problems of computer perception unless the machine in question has peripherals for receiving aural or visual information, which the QL docs not yet have. However, we can look at some of the fundamental features of finding patterns in input. Whether the input is words typed in at a keyboard or images received by a video camera the problems are very much the same.

6.2 Spelling and style

We can begin with a simple example, spelling. Most computers run word processors and most users of word processors make spelling mistakes. It is therefore useful to have a program which can check your spelling for you and tell you what the correct spelling should be if you have made an error.

In essence such a program is very simple. It consists of a dictionary of patterns (i.e., character strings) and compares each word in your word-processed text against the nearest entries in the dictionary. So it takes a pattern from the text, looks for the nearest pattern in the dictionary and if it finds a pattern that matches exactly it regards it as a correct spelling and moves to the next word. If you have any difficulty imagining how this could be done a simple example is used in the synonym program in Chapter 8.

This is pattern matching at its simplest. Each item of input is compared with all possible patterns held in the list of patterns and if an input pattern does not match one in the dictionary it is regarded as an error. It may not be an error, of course. American spelling checkers often treat 'colour' as a spelling mistake because it is not in their dictionaries. However, good spelling checkers will allow you to alter the dictionary and add your own items.

A more significant problem is the spelling error which is actually a mistake but is held in the dictionary. Suppose, for example, I typed 'I through the ball at the teacher'. This is obviously the wrong spelling of 'through'. (To be pedantic it is not a wrong spelling but choice of the wrong one of two homophones.) The spelling checker will not notice this because, as far as it is concerned, 'through' is in the dictionary so it is correctly spelt.

However, if the dictionary also contained a representation of the patterns in which such a pattern could occur, many such problems would be overcome. Of course it would be impossible to list all the contexts in which such a spelling error might occur, but we could look for rules of language use which might describe the likely context. One obvious rule that would apply in the above example is that the 'through/threw' in the sentence should be a verb. We know this because it occurs immediately after one noun group, immediately before another and there is otherwise no verb in the sentence. So if 'threw' was marked not only as a pattern of characters but also indexed as 'occurs only in slots where one would expect a verb', whilst 'through' is coded as 'occurs in an adjunct after a verb of motion', then the spelling checker would know that the wrong spelling had been used.

To generalize the point for a moment, so that it applies to pattern matching in perception at all levels of input, a pattern is not just a structure of elements. A word is not just a string of characters. It may also be part of a larger pattern and it may itself be made up of elements which themselves have structures and patterns. Herein lies a major problem in pattern matching. It is not good enough just to match the pattern at one level of correspondence. It must match at all levels to be properly understood.

Let us take the example a little further. It is possible to create programs which do more than just check spelling of a text. They can also carry out stylistic analyses, leading to judgements like 'You have used the passive too frequently for non-scientific writing and it is unusual to find such a high proportion of abstractions in writing for a non-technical audience. You have a poor readability index which probably means that your sentences are too long and you have used jargon where more familiar terms would be more appropriate.' Bell laboratories have developed a package called 'Writer's Workbench' which does this kind of work and IBM are in the final stages of a similar program called 'Epistle'.

To arrive at such a judgement, which is very much the kind of thing teachers of English language might say about a piece of writing, a program does at least two things. Firstly it looks at various files of patterns that it holds. For example, in order to make the judgement about abstract nouns it looks for instances of a pattern ending in -ion (such as 'consideration', 'obfuscation', 'clarification'). Secondly it counts all the instances of the patterns it finds. It then takes the totals for each of the patterns and compares them with a list of rules that it holds and uses the rules to make judgements. One such rule might be 'If more than 20 per cent of the nouns are abstract and the subject matter is not philosophy then the degree of abstraction is too high.'

It is therefore looking for patterns which it expects to find and is making judgements accordingly. However, all such judgements have to be made in the light of each other. For example, how would the program know whether the subject matter of the text was philosophy or not? It would have a dictionary of words and phrases commonly found in philosophical discourse and, if it found more than a certain percentage, it would be able to conclude that the text was philosophical.

Unless, of course, the text was actually a satire on a philosophical discourse, or a review of a book about philosophy, or a poem using philosophy as a sustained metaphor. In these cases it would have to make exceptions, which means it would have to find out whether the text was a poem or a satire, etc. To do this it would have other lists of patterns and other rules, and some of those might relate to the number of abstract nouns.

To generalize again, we have here the second problem of pattern matching. The evidence that leads to one conclusion may be contradicted by other evidence. The same evidence may be used in different ways and conclusions at one stage in the decision-making process may distort decisions made later on. It is often impossible to reach certain conclusions, so pattern-matching programs have to arrive at a balance of probabilities, just as expert systems must draw probabilistic conclusions from possibly contradictory evidence. Ultimately it all depends on that nebulous phenomenon, context.

6.3 Speech acts

Let us now change tack a little and consider the problem which keeps occurring, that of context. Mistakes, misinformation and communication breakdowns are often the result of not realizing the relevant context for a given pattern. Many visual illusions work because the eye is not given sufficient context in which to make a decision, or because the context has been distorted to induce faulty conditions. The simple illusion reproduced in Fig. 6.1, whereby two lines of equal length appear different, results from the

Figure 6.1

context of receding diagonal lines in which they are placed. The eye decodes the diagonals as an indication of perspective. So, the brain says, if this is a perspective drawing, as those diagonal lines tell me it is, and I know things in the distance are smaller, the line at the rear must be longer than the line at the front. Of course there is no 'front' and 'rear' because you are actually looking at a flat page and the lines are the same length. But the brain inevitably sees such drawings in the context of railway lines and sleepers and so veers towards misunderstanding.

Getting around such perceptual problems is, for human beings, a question of hard visual training. Being a visual artist is mainly about learning to see what is 'really' there rather than what habit makes us think is there. For computers such training is harder because we have no easy way of telling it what relevant context actually is.

Let us return to the example of text processing. Suppose we have a program that can parse sentences and can assign meanings correctly to all the words in the sentence (quite a large suppose). The computer may still not be able to understand the overall meaning of the sentence because it has an imperfect understanding of the context in which it occurred. For example, if it receives the sentence 'If Jim shouts at me again I will give him a thick ear.' We know that is a threat. But how might a computer come to the same conclusion? The context will be a major clue. If Jim and the speaker do not like each other, if the speaker is more powerful than Jim, if Jim shouts a lot, if the speaker does not like shouting and if Jim does not like thick ears, then it is likely that the sentence is a threat rather than, say, a prediction or a promise.

This brings us to the notion of speech acts. A major advance in recent artificial intelligence work was the realization that speech acts are a powerful way of describing the context of utterances for computers. A speech act is quite simply what it says—an act which is performed by using speech. There are only one or two ways to threaten someone and the main one is through speech. There is only one way to get married and that is by carrying out the speech act of 'vowing' (saying I do). If the vicar says 'Do you take this woman to be your lawful wedded wife' and the answer is 'I suppose so' it does not count. It is necessary to say 'I do' and only that speech act can produce the desired result.

In fact most language is a speech act of some kind. All questions can be thought of as a statement beginning 'I request that . . .'. All statements can be thought of as beginning 'I state that . . .'. All orders can be thought of as beginning 'I order you to . . .'. If this is so, then if the computer can be taught to recognize particular speech acts it has a major clue to the context and thus to assigning an unambiguous meaning to any input phrase. Fortunately many (not all) speech acts are signalled by patterns of one kind or another.

6.4 Threat

The program shown as Fig. 6.2 recognizes threats. It does this by looking for a pattern in an input text. The pattern is encoded in line 240, which says in translation: 'If the tense of the verb is future and there is a hostile word in the sentence and the relation expressed in the sentence is such that the speaker is the subject of the sentence and the hearer is the object of the sentence, then regard the sentence as a threat.' The program does not look simply for one clue, such as the word threat, it looks for the coincidence of all the above conditions. All are necessary for a sentence to be a threat.

```
100 REM Program to recognise a threat
110 RESTORE
120 CLS
130 init
140 PRINT "Type in a sentence"
150 INPUT sentence$
160 threat_test
170 STOP
180 :
190 DEFine PROCedure threat_test
200 then_pos= " then " INSTR sentence$
210 consequence$=sentence$(then_pos+4 TO LEN(sentence$))
220 wd=verb_act(consequence$)
230 IF wd=0 THEN PRINT"No verb":RETurn
240 IF tense=fut AND hostile(wd)=true AND relation(speaker$(consequence$),hearer$(consequence$),consequence$)= true THEN
250 PRINT "Is that a threat?"
260 ELSE
270 PRINT "okay"
280 END IF
290 END DEFine threat_test
300 :
```

Figure 6.2 (*continues*)

```
310 DEFine FuNction tense
320 RETurn word(wd,tn)
330 END DEFine tense
340 :
350 DEFine FuNction hostile(wd)
360 RETurn word(wd,hostility)
370 END DEFine hostile
380 :
390 DEFine FuNction verb_act(text$)
400 FOR i = 1 TO 10
410 verb_pos= word$(i) INSTR text$
420 IF verb_pos <>0 THEN RETurn i:EXIT i
430 NEXT i
440 RETurn 0
450 END FOR i
460 END DEFine verb_act
470 :
480 DEFine FuNction relation(su$,ob$,text$)
490 IF subject(su$,text$)=true AND object(ob$,text$)=true THEN
500 RETurn true
510 ELSE
520 RETurn false
530 END IF
540 END DEFine relation
550 :
560 DEFine FuNction speaker$(text$)
570 IF " I " INSTR text$ <>0 THEN
580 RETurn " I "
590 ELSE
600 IF " my " INSTR text$ <>0 THEN
610 RETurn " my "
620 ELSE
630 RETurn " dummy "
640 END IF
650 END IF
660 END DEFine speaker$
670 :
```

Figure 6.2 (*continues*)

```
680 DEFine FuNction hearer$(text$)
690  IF " you " INSTR text$ <>0 THEN
700    RETurn " you "
710  ELSE
720    IF " your " INSTR text$ <>0 THEN
730      RETurn " your "
740    ELSE
750      RETurn "dummy"
760    END IF
770  END IF
780 END DEFine hearer$
790 :
800 DEFine FuNction subject(t1$,t2$)
810  IF t1$ INSTR t2$ < verb_pos THEN
820    RETurn true
830  ELSE
840    RETurn false
850  END IF
860 END DEFine subject
870 :
880 DEFine FuNction object(t1$,t2$)
890  IF t1$ INSTR t2$ > verb_pos THEN
900    RETurn true
910  ELSE
920    RETurn false
930  END IF
940 END DEFine object
950 :
960 DEFine PROCedure init
970  DIM word$(10,20)
980  DIM word(10,2)
990  FOR i=1 TO 10
1000   READ word$(i),word(i,1),word(i,2)
1010 NEXT i
1020 fut=1
1030 false=0
1040 true=1
1050 hostility=1
```

Figure 6.2 (*continues*)

```
1060 tn=2
1070 END DEFine init
1080 :
1090 DATA "will kick",1,1
1100 DATA "will demote",1,1
1110 DATA "will murder",1,1
1120 DATA "might hate",1,1
1130 DATA "won't mind",0,1
1140 DATA "was angry",1,-1
1150 DATA "am angry",1,0
1160 DATA "will complain",1,1
1170 DATA "will smile",0,1
1180 DATA "will pay",0,1
```

Figure 6.2

A sentence does not count as a threat if it is not about the future because threats are concerned with things that will or might happen. A sentence is not a threat if the future action is not hostile (or at least unwelcome) to the hearer. Nor is it a threat (in most cases) if the hearer is not the object of the sentence. This is actually a weaker condition because it is possible to threaten to perform an action which will affect the hearer without mentioning him/her, as in 'If you don't be good I will sell the QL'. This would be a threat to me, because I like my QL and want to keep it, but I am not mentioned in the second clause.

The program works as a series of embedded functions. The main routine simply calls the set-up routine, obtains a sentence and then tests to see if that sentence is a threat. Initialization is straightforward. Two arrays are set up: one (word$) holds the verb phrases; the other holds in its first dimension a code representing the hostility and in its second a code representing the tense of that verb. Hostility is simply a binary flag—1 for a hostile verb, 0 for a neutral or friendly one. A real application would require a more sensitive representation as some verbs are only hostile to certain types of people or in certain situations. Tense is also simplified into past, −1, present, 0, and future, +1. Only ten verb phrases are given but these could be supplemented.

Procedure threat__test firstly establishes that the word 'then' occurs in the sentence. If it does not, the sentence is not regarded as a threat. However, the presence of 'then' is not sufficient as promises and guesses can also use the word. The remaining tests apply only to the clause after 'then'. This means that the program can recognize a very large number of different threats, as the sentence up to 'then' can be any meaningful string. The first portion of the sentence can be regarded as the 'condition' and the second one as the 'consequence'.

Next we establish if the verb used in the consequence is in the dictionary and if so which verb it is. Procedure verb__act does this by simply testing to see if any of the words in the dictionary are also in consequence$ and returning the value of any verb found. If no verb is found (i.e., wd = 0) then an error message is printed and the program ends. Note that only the ten verbs held in the dictionary count as verbs and you will have to add any others you think likely to occur.

Having found a verb function, tense returns the tense of that verb. There is actually no reason to use a function to carry out this test except to make the testing line, 240, hold an English-like representation of the operations being carried out. Function hostile tells us if the verb has a hostility index of 1. Function relation tests to see if the speaker in consequence$ is the subject and if the hearer in consequence$ is the object. As its parameters are themselves functions which return true if the first person pronoun and the second person pronoun are present in the sentence, they are evaluated first and the words they return are passed as parameters to two further functions, subject and object, which return true if the word occurs before the verb in the case of the first person and after the verb in the case of the second person. If all these tests are true, then the sentence is regarded as a threat and an appropriate message is printed.

There are several reasons for all these functions. One is an attempt to make the actual tests look more like what is actually going on rather than simply the manipulation of a series of numbers. For demonstration purposes this is a good idea as it can be thought of as a representation of 'thought processes' and this is much easier to understand if words rather than numbers are the items being manipulated.

Secondly this provides a small introduction to the way that a function-based language works. Function-based languages are common in artificial intelligence programming because they represent closely some of the actual logic of the design being coded. Logic programming using Prolog and list processing using LISP are both built around the idea that intelligence involves the manipulation of meaningful symbols rather than abstract counters.

Finally these functions provide an example of how SuperBASIC allows functions to be parameters in other functions, so that complex embedded nests of logic can be built which evaluate to just one value. However, remember that a function does not necessarily evaluate to only one of two values. Line 240 has been constructed so that the whole thing evaluates to either true or false, but SuperBASIC regards any value which is not 0 as true, so at some level in your logic you must have primitive functions which restrict the available range of responses to two—true (represented here as 1) and false (=0). All decisions can be broken down into a series of binary decisions, so logic programming of this kind is possible in SuperBASIC, but some people will regard it as cumbersome and unnecessary because of the extra levels of analysis it imposes. However, these extra levels are half the point of logic programming because they expose the fundamental nature of the problems being analysed.

6.5 Speech

One of the most fundamental features of language is that it is spoken. As part of the aim of AI is to create computers which are more like human beings, it seems important that such machines have the ability to produce speech and to understand it. Of course both these aspects involve all the other features of language discussed elsewhere in this book—the computer must be able to recognize and produce grammatical, sensible and appropriate utterances and to understand such utterances. But speech involves the additional problem of being able to process and produce sounds. And speech is one of the most complex patterns that human beings process.

Just as written languages use an alphabet of characters to represent meanings, so spoken languages use a list of sounds out of which larger patterned units such as syllables, words and sentences can be formed. Exactly what you call these sounds depends on the perspective you are adopting, but it is common to talk about 'phonemes' or 'allophones'. In most dialects of English there are about 45 phonemes used to form all normal speech. Each phoneme is distinct from all other phonemes and speakers of a language recognize this by knowing, for example, that the /p/ phoneme and the /b/ phoneme change the meaning of an otherwise identical string of sounds. For example, the string represented as /-ig/ has a different meaning depending on which of the two phonemes fill the vacant slot. If the pattern /-ig/ has the first slot filled by /b/ the result is a different word than would result if it is filled by /p/.

However, there are some differences of sound that can be used in a language but do not change meaning. For example, the /l/ sound in 'full' is quite different from the /l/ sound in 'flee'. If you say these words aloud you will find that the back of your tongue is raised towards the rear of your mouth in the first case but in the second case the tip of your tongue is raised nearer to the front of your mouth. The first sound is often called 'dark l' and the second sound 'clear l'. They are definitely different sounds produced in different ways, but they do not affect meaning. They are both 'l' sounds. In a similar way the Japanese language treats the /l/ sound and the /r/ sound as indistinguishable variants of the same sound which do not change meaning.

Two sounds which are different and whose choice changes meaning are called phonemes. Two sounds which are different but which do not change meaning and are regarded by speakers of the language as the same sound are called 'allophones'. Because the difference between two allophones or phonemes is often only on a single dimension it is quite easy to represent such sounds digitally. For example the sounds /p/ and /b/ are produced by exactly the same movements of the tongue and lips. The only difference between them (and therefore the only difference between the spoken words 'pig' and 'big') is that /b/ uses a vibration in the throat and /p/ does not. If you say these sounds aloud with your hand against your throat you can feel the vibration produced by /b/ which is lacking for /p/. This vibration, called 'voicing', is also the only difference between /t/ and /d/, /s/ and /z/, /k/ and /g/ and some other pairs of sounds.

As we can represent such sounds as collections of features which they either possess or do not possess we can represent them digitally. For example, a reasonably full definition of /p/ which distinguishes it from all other English phonemes is 'a voiceless bilabial plosive'. Compare this with /b/ which is 'a voiced bilabial plosive' or /k/ which is 'a voiceless alveolar fricative' or /g/ which is 'a voiced alveolar fricative'. These linguistic jargon words simply distinguish between sounds produced with the lips or with the alveolar ridge, and between sounds produced by completely obstructing air for a moment, hence producing an 'explosion' or 'plosive', and those which do not completely obstruct air, producing friction or a 'fricative'.

If we set up a table which holds the distinctions:

voiced/voiceless
bilabial/alveolar
plosive/fircative,

then we can distinguish between these four sounds completely in a digital way. Suppose we represent the left-hand side of the table as 0 and the right-hand side as 1, then /p/ is 100, /b/ is 000, /k/ is 111 and /g/ is 011.

Now, providing we can produce very small units of sound corresponding to voicing, friction and explosion, we can digitally produce the sounds of English by combining these basic elements in different ways.

Unfortunately the sound chips of most micros do not provide enough control adequately to reproduce these minute chunks of sound. Nor is it quite as simple as it seems here, because the criteria for distinguishing sounds are not quite as symmetrical as I have suggested. However, the principle of digital synthesis of sounds is well understood and most micros can be given add-on boards or chips which allow you to produce words by allophone synthesis.

The alternative approach to speech generation is less versatile. Instead of storing only information on allophones and adding strings of allophones together to produce words, whole words are stored on ROM. The principles behind synthesis of complete words are the same but the user or programmer does not need to go through the difficult business of analysing language into its basic components. However, ROM-based vocabulary is usually quite small and pretty inflexible, a common penalty for convenience.

When such add-ons are available, however, it is a very simple matter to replace the written data used in any of the programs in this book with allophonic representations, and thus bring your micro one step closer to becoming an 'intelligent' machine. But even when such boards are around there will still be problems of speech production which prevent digital speech from coming close to natural human speech.

The greatest of these is also a problem for speech recognition systems. Speech recognition is a much harder technology to implement than speech production because instead of using discrete digital signals to produce a version of a continuous analogue waveform we have to do the reverse. We have to take a real wave of sound, which has no real digital elements, and convert it into a digital representation which somehow accurately represents the spoken sounds.

The difficulty should be clear if you remember that our description of speech production depends on how the vocal organs are used to produce a sound rather than the actual nature of the sound itself. Clearly a given phoneme is actually produced by friction or it is not, a digital description. But actual sounds once they have been articulated are not discrete phenomena. Speech synthesis technology is actually 'articulation' technology. It simulates discrete positions of the vocal organs. Speech recognition technology is acoustic technology. It has to decipher the raw sounds themselves and these are complex and continuous waveforms.

Crucial to such waveforms is intonation. Intonation is a kind of contour of pitch which is laid over the basic sounds of a language. It is not really a digital phenomenon, though it can be simplified and described in roughly digital ways. It is very difficult, however, to describe the digital structure of an allophone together with the overlay of the part of the intonation contour which that allophone is carrying on a particular occasion. This is because intonation can be so marked that it can totally change the basic characteristics of the allophone. For example, clear /l/ may be changed to dark /l/ or even /p/ can sound almost like /b/.

Once again we return to the problem of context. Human beings understand such 'distorted' allophones because of the context in which they occur. As a simple example, you are unlikely to hear anyone say 'The farmer fed the bigs.' Because of the context you will interpret such a sequence as 'The farmer fed the pigs.' Perhaps on first reading you even read the sentence printed here as 'pigs' or thought it was a misprint. We use very complex rules of context in decoding what we hear. We do not just use the raw sounds. But computers only have the raw sounds to play with, so they find it very hard to decide if a particular chunk of sound is actually the phoneme /b/ or /p/ with a heavy intonation.

Adding exact intonation to speech production and recognizing speech accurately depends on being able to represent context in a form that a computer can understand and process. For this reason digital sound synthesis on its own cannot produce human speech. It depends very much on developing adequate software techniques for representing the meanings of the surrounding context and, more importantly, developing routines for recognizing what is important or relevant in that context. We will return to this later in the book when we consider the nature of semantics, databases and memory. There remains one further example of pattern matching to look at where AI may be very effective—translation.

6.6 Machine translation

One use for computers which seemed obvious even in the 1950s was to translate texts from one language to another. It was argued that a computer is not really a number processor but a symbol processor, and therefore it should be easy to write programs which translate the symbols of one language into those of another. A great deal of money and effort was spent trying to achieve this in the fifties and sixties, but success was very limited. Computer scientists just had not realized that translation is a task that requires some of the characteristics we regard as intelligence. It is not simply a process of finding a word in a dictionary of English, looking the equivalent word up in the dictionary of another language and writing it down, as any professional translator will tell you. Consider, for example, the following algorithm:

1. input sentence in English;
2. for each word in sentence:
3. isolate word,
4. find its number in English dictionary,
5. find French word with corresponding number,
6. print French word;
7. if any words left, go to (2).

This algorithm assumes several things which are not actually true. Firstly that there is a one-to-one correspondence between words in one language and words in another such that for every word in language (a) there is one and only one word in language (b) which has the same meaning (i.e., the same 'number' in our algorithm). Secondly it assumes that translation is only a business of translating word meanings. As we have seen, words are not the only things with meaning in language. Other structures also carry meaning. Sounds, phrases, bits of words (morphemes) and clauses all have structures of their own and meanings of their own. An accurate translation from one language to another must take in all the levels of language.

There is also, once again, the problem of cultural specificity or context. A famous example of mistranslation is the translation of the idiomatic English phrase 'Out of sight, out of mind' into Russian and back again into English. The result was 'Invisible idiot'. Literally, of course, this is a perfectly reasonable translation. If something is out of sight it could be said to be invisible, and an idiot is someone who is out of his mind. But this particular combination of words has a special meaning which only someone familiar with English-speaking culture and all its many peculiarities would know. It means it needs a complex decision algorithm.

In order for a program like the above to cope with such difficulties it would need not only a dictionary of words but also of all phrases and idioms which have meanings one could not immediately deduce from that combination of words. In addition the program would have to know when to look at the idiom dictionary and when to look at the single-word dictionary, which means it needs to complex decision algorithm.

But this is not all. If we were to translate the phrase 'Out of sight, out of mind' thoroughly we would have to give some of its flavour also, because it has a certain 'aesthetic' or 'poetic' appeal. One of the main reasons idiomatic phrases are preserved in a language is that they 'sound nice'. People remember them not only because they aptly summarize a particular meaning but also because they are pleasing to the ear (and also because it is easier to remember a highly structured phrase than an unstructured one). The 'poetic' qualities of our phrase lie in its repetition of structures, namely two groups of three words, each group beginning with the same two words. In addition the third word in each group has the same vowel (a diphthong), a relationship normally known as assonance. So if we were to translate this phrase 'properly' rather than just to give its gist, the translation would have to result in a two-part phrase containing repetition of words and assonance. This is a tall order for a human translator, let alone an electrical one.

The efficacy of a machine translator is therefore a function of what you want it to do. The more faithful you want it to be to the original the more intelligence it has to have. Simple word-for-word translation is relatively easy (but even here context can be vital when, for example, distinguishing between the meanings of 'count' in 'The Count of Monte Cristo', 'Count these beads' and 'What is the head count?'). Adding syntactic complexity involves parsing and text-creation routines like the ones we have considered elsewhere in this book. Adding context and idioms is well-nigh impossible.

However, machine translators are in use and developing their flexibility is one of the aims of current fifth-generation projects. 'Phrasebook' translators are already available, some of them with spoken output. These are no more than the dictionary look-up routines described in our little algorithm, with all the limitations of vocabulary and flexibility that this implies. Their advantages over traditional phrasebooks are simply the immediate access to data and the speech output which gives you not only the words but also the pronunciation.

More sophisticated machine translators are used by some political and business organizations. These are built with certain constraints, notably that they should only be expected to work in specific areas (such as, for example, academic articles on nuclear physics). This ensures that the vocabulary does not have to be enormous, that idiomatic or jargon phrases can be listed and kept in an appropriate dictionary and that when mistakes are made the context can often resolve difficulties. For example, if a program had difficulty translating the word 'charm' it would conclude that the meaning 'attraction of subatomic particles' is more likely than 'pleasant human personality' because of the context.

But the second major constraint is that the real translation is still done by human beings. Systems vary but the basic process is:

1. Take the text in language (a) and run a program on it to translate it. Output is a version of the language which is unambiguous. This may even be an 'artificial' formal language. Where the program cannot make a certain decision let it report all possible interpretations.

2. A human operator, expert in language (a), goes through the translation resolving all the problems and ambiguities by using her or his intuitive knowledge of the language.
3. A second program is run on the resulting unambiguous representation to produce a text in language (b). When more than one possible translation of a word or phrase is possible all possibilities are given.
4. A human expert in language (b) goes through the translation resolving problems and ambiguities until an acceptable language (b) text results.

Such a system recognizes the limitations of machine intelligence. The real intelligence comes here from the human operators who resolve ambiguities and solve problems. However, it can be a significantly useful tool because it removes much of the repetitive and mechanical procedures from translation which leaves human beings to face the more interesting tasks. It is also possible to run such systems without either human operator knowing much about both languages, because the role of the operator is primarily to interpret existing clumsy texts in their own languages. In some cases the ambiguity can be resolved only by recourse to the original version in the original language, but in many it is clear to a native speaker what the meaning should be even if they do not know a single word of the original text.

Constructing a translation system on a micro faces the problems of commercial systems and can only approach them in the same ways. You should design the basic system around word-to-word translation, each word being marked for its syntactic value using a parser like the ATN grammar described above. This will give a number of possible parses stringing a number of possible meanings together. A human operator should then select one of those possible strings as being the best representation of the input text.

This representation can then be fed to a separate program which takes an ATN description of a sentence and places words of another language into the appropriate slots. For example, if the representation starts with a noun phrase, then the program should first construct a noun phrase (or its equivalent) in the second language. It should do so by finding all words in its dictionary which have the meaning of the words held in the representation and constructing all the legitimate noun phrases that those words can generate.

Having proceeded in this way through the whole of the input text it can continue in one of two ways. Either it can output all of the many sentences it has constructed in language (b) and let the user choose between them or (and probably a better strategy) it can output each substructure at each stage of creation, allowing the user to choose the best of all the current possibilities.

To put some intelligence into such a pair of programs, tests would need to be added that replaced some of the user's evaluation. For example, the first program could request a description of the context of the translation, offering the user a limited number of possibilities which represented the vocabulary it was equipped to cope with. For example, it might say 'Choose academic or non-academic. Choose one of "physics, chemistry and biology".' Then in the process of choosing possible representations, it would automatically reject any meanings not marked in the dictionary as being in the appropriate context. Naturally some words could be marked as belonging to all the possible fields, some to only one. Such an approach is fine in a limited application but there are so many possible contexts that a dictionary to cope with all styles and registers simply could not be created.

As is usual in AI the tests which are incorporated would have to be equivalent to the kinds of checks that human beings employ when they translate, so the effectiveness (and intelligence) of such a translating suite would depend on how well the process of translation had been understood by the programmer and/or designer. As I have already said, there are still many aspects of language which are imperfectly understood, so if you are planning to write such a program, you should recognize both that you will not be able to do everything you hope to do but that there is also a possibility that you may discover something new in the attempt.

7 Memory

7.1 Human memory

If we are going to make computers reason we need them to remember things, and if we want them to reason like human beings it may make sense to make them remember like human beings. The trouble is (and you are probably expecting this by now) psychologists do not really know how people do remember things or how some aspects of memory work.

In some ways human memory and computer memory seem similar. For example, just as computers typically have ROM, which is permanent memory, and RAM, which is temporary memory, so human beings have what is called long-term memory and short-term memory. Short-term memory seems to be able to hold only a few pieces of information at a time and quickly loses that information. Long-term memory, on the other hand, can retain information for many years, perhaps for an entire human life.

But all computer memory operates in the same way. If you need to put something into, or take something out of, computer memory you need to know the address of the memory location you want to write to or read from. You cannot manipulate any of the computer memory without knowing and manipulating addresses. But it seems that information is stored in human memory in complex and interwoven ways. Some information may be recovered by knowing the 'address' to look for. However, most information in our minds seems to be linked to other information in quite unusual ways. In some cases a particular piece of data in memory is regarded as a piece of information, recoverable as data, a fragment of memory, but on other occasions, when accessed by a different route through the mind it becomes a pointer—not data at all but a signpost indicating another memory. Everyone knows how one memory leads to another and how there are different strategies for searching memory for a given piece of information, sometimes resulting in forgotten fragments being 'brought to mind'. There is some evidence to suggest that these subjective feelings are linked to actual neurological phenomena.

So in our minds the same piece of data can sometimes be data and sometimes be an index to other data. In a computer a piece of data can seldom be regarded both as address and data. A clever programmer would be able to design some of his storage data so that addresses could also be data, but only in very special programming circumstances. So if we want to simulate human memory we will have to create special data structures which represent the kinds of links which (probably) exist in human memory.

7.2 Synonym chains

The simplest kind of link between memory items might be where one item points to another item of a similar kind. For example, all words which have similar meanings might point to all other words with the same meanings. For a computer it would be inefficient for every word to point to every other word with the same meaning but the data can be arranged in such a way that each word points to one word with the same meaning, that word points to the next and so on down the line until the final item which points back to the first item in the list.

Such an arrangement could be regarded as a continuous chain of data, an endless loop of related items. The program below (Fig. 7.1) demonstrates just such a simple data structure. Procedure init first creates a small database of adjectives encoding various aspects of objects such as size, colour and age. For each of these semantic aspects there are several adjectives held in the array adj$. A second array, point, holds a pointer corresponding to each adjective which points to another adjective with the same meaning. The data to be placed in these arrays is held in the data statements from line 930 onwards. It would be a simple matter to add more lines holding more data of the same kind providing the arrays are made larger (they are created in line 240) and the control variable i in line 250 is incremented to the maximum size of the arrays. However, this version of Synonym is limited to 26 adjectives.

After the database has been created procedure text requests a sentence which contains an adjective. Line 340 adds a space to the input sentence so that all words end with spaces.

Procedure findadj then loops through the input string (text$) one word at a time and compares the current word with all the items in the dictionary. A word is extracted from the text by the well-known method of regarding all characters between two spaces as a word. This is not a foolproof method because users may type spaces by mistake, may put two spaces next to each other or may include punctuation, but for our demonstrative purposes it is good enough.

Firstly a temporary string called xt$ is created which is given the input string (line 380). This is necessary because xt$ will be altered, but we need to

```
100 CLS
110 init
120 REPeat control
130   text
140   findadj
150   IF adj<>0 THEN EXIT control
160   PRINT "You have not used an adjective in my dictionary"
170 END REPeat control
180 chooseadj
190 output
200 STOP
210 :
220 DEFine PROCedure init
230   RESTORE
240   DIM adj$(26,16),pointer(26)
250   FOR i=1 TO 26
260     READ adj$(i)
270     READ pointer(i)
280   NEXT i
290 END DEFine init
300 :
310 DEFine PROCedure text
320   PRINT "Please type a sentence which uses an adjective"
330   INPUT text$
340   text$=text$&" "
350 END DEFine text
360 :
370 DEFine PROCedure findadj
380   xt$=text$
390   REPeat loop
400     sp= " " INSTR xt$
410     word$= xt$(1 TO sp)
420     word$=word$(1 TO LEN(word$)-1)
430     adj=0
440     FOR i=1 TO 26
450       IF word$=adj$(i) THEN adj=i
460     NEXT i
```

Figure 7.1 (*continues*)

```
470 IF adj<>0 THEN
480 sent1$=text$(1 TO LEN(text$)-LEN(xt$))
490 sent2$=xt$(sp TO LEN(xt$))
500 EXIT loop
510 ELSE
520 IF sp<> LEN(xt$) THEN
530 xt$=xt$(sp+1 TO LEN(xt$))
540 ELSE
550 xt$=""
560 END IF
570 END IF
580 IF xt$="" THEN EXIT loop
590 END REPeat loop
600 END DEFine findadj
610 :
620 DEFine PROCedure chooseadj
630 REPeat decide
640 r=RND(8)
650 x=0
660 p=adj
670 REPeat inloop
680 x=x+1
690 p=pointer(p)
700 IF x>=r THEN EXIT inloop
710 END REPeat inloop
720 IF p<>adj THEN EXIT decide
730 END REPeat decide
740 adj=p
750 END DEFine chooseadj
760 :
770 DEFine PROCedure output
780 PRINT "I think:"
790 art
800 PRINT \sent1$;adj$(adj);sent2$
810 PRINT\"means the same as:"
820 PRINT \text$
830 END DEFine output
840 :
850 DEFine PROCedure art
```

Figure 7.1 (*continues*)

```
860 IF sentl$(LEN(sentl$)-2 TO LEN(sentl$))=" a "
    AND adj$(adj,1) INSTR "@aeiou" >1 THEN
870 sentl$=sentl$(1 TO LEN(sentl$)-1)&"n "
880 END IF
890 IF sentl$(LEN(sentl$)-2 TO LEN(sentl$))="an "
AND adj$(adj,1) INSTR "@aeiou" <2 THEN
900 sentl$=sentl$(1 TO LEN(sentl$)-2)&" "
910 END IF
920 END DEFine art
930 :
940 DATA "big",2
950 DATA "large",3
960 DATA "huge",4
970 DATA "enormous",1
980 DATA "small",6
990 DATA "tiny",7
1000 DATA "little",8
1010 DATA "minute",5
1020 DATA "dark",10
1030 DATA "black",11
1040 DATA "inky",9
1050 DATA "red",13
1060 DATA "ruby",14
1070 DATA "poppy coloured",15
1080 DATA "scarlet",12
1090 DATA "blue",17
1100 DATA "azure",18
1110 DATA "aquamarine",19
1120 DATA "sky-blue",16
1130 DATA "old",21
1140 DATA "aged",22
1150 DATA "antique",23
1160 DATA "veteran",20
1170 DATA "young",25
1180 DATA "immature",26
1190 DATA "youthful",24
```

Figure 7.1

remember the original string in its entirety for the output. The first space in xt$ is found using INSTR (line 400) and all characters between the beginning of xt$ and the position of the space are placed in the variable word$. This is the current word to be compared. Line 420 then removes the space from word$. Lines 430 and 460 count through the entire dictionary of 26 words (remember to change the control variable in line 440 if you alter the size of the array). If word$ is the same as any adjective in the dictionary, then a flag called adj is set to the array element in which the adjective is held.

Lines 470 and 570 carry out one of two actions, depending on whether a match for word$ has been found. If it has, then adj is equal to a value other than zero so this is tested in line 470. If true, then the original input text is divided into two portions. The first portion is the input string up to the beginning of the word currently being looked at. As this is equivalent to the current first character of xt$ all that is necessary is to subtract the length of xt$ from text$ to give the number of characters in text$ which occur before word$. These are held in a new string variable, sentl$. Similarly sent2$ holds everything in xt$ after the current word. The effect, of course, is to extract the current word from text$ and hold the two parts in two string variables. Finally control exits from the testing loop because we do not need to test any further words to find an adjective.

One consequence of doing it this way is that only the first adjective in the dictionary is acted upon. If you wanted a program which found synonyms for all the adjectives (assuming the input sentence contained more than one) then this testing loop would have to be continued until all words had been tested and the input string would have to be cut up into as many substrings as there were adjectives in the input. In such a case a better strategy would probably be to hold all input words individually as elements of an array (as we did in the ATN parser) so that those which were found in the dictionary could be automatically substituted. As this version of Synonym is only concerned with single adjectives such an approach would be wasteful.

What if the current word does not match with any item in the dictionary? This is the ELSE case of lines 510 and 570. Firstly another test must be made to see if we have come to the end of the input string. This will be the case if the position of the next space is also the number of characters in xt$. If we are not at the end of xt$ then xt$ is reduced by the length of the current word, otherwise xt$ becomes an empty string (line 550).

If xt$ becomes an empty string there are no more words to compare with the dictionary. In other words, no adjectives were found. So we leave the loop and return to the main procedure. Here line 150 checks to see if an adjective was found. If adj is not equal to zero, then we leap out of the loop called 'control'. Otherwise an error message is printed and the loop cycles back to procedure text to ask for another sentence.

Once an adjective has been found procedure chooseadj uses a synonym chain to select another adjective. This is done simply. Firstly a random number, r, is selected up to a maximum of 8. (There is no reason why eight was chosen, it could be any value providing it is larger than the length of the longest synonym chain.) The REPEAT loop called inloop will now cycle round r times. It begins with p, a value initially equal to adj (i.e., the address of the adjective in the database). A control variable x is then incremented by one and p is changed to the value held in the array called pointer for that adjective. In other words p is used as a pointer into the array called pointer, and it is then changed to the value of the element in the array that it points to. This means that it will now point to a different element in both arrays, i.e., a different adjective.

The procedure is simply repeated over and over again. Variable x is incremented and p is changed to the value of the element it currently points to. This continues until $x \rangle = r$ (line 700) when we exit from inloop. Now p has the value of an element in adj$ which is a synonym of the input adjective. However, it may, by accident, hold the value of that adjective because the cycle may have ended up pointing back to the initial element. So we need to test to ensure that p is now not equal to adj (line 720). If they are the same, then we go through the whole business again. However, if p and adj are now different we exit from the outer loop, called decide, set adj to its new value (p) and return to the main routine.

Now all that remains is to print out the strings sent1$ and sent2$ with the new adjective between them. This is procedure output. But there is one further problem we must deal with. Both the input adjective and its synonym may begin with consonants or they may both begin with vowels, in which case the article ('a' or 'an') will not need changing. But if one of them begins with a vowel and the other does not then the article has to be changed. This is a small point perhaps but it is the kind of thing that makes a significant difference between output that just plays with text and output that has some semblance of intelligence.

Procedure art therefore sorts this out. Quite simply it carries out two tests. The first (lines 860 to 880) says 'If the last bit of sent1$ is "a" and the adjective begins with a vowel, then add an "n" to sent1$'. The second test says 'If the last bit of sent1$ is "an" and the adjective does not begin with a vowel then take the "n" from sent1$'.

You will see that there is scope for improvement in this program. In the first place if the input adjective is not in the small dictionary the program can do nothing but ask for a further sentence. As it uses some of the most common adjectives the user is quite likely to type one of the items held, but this is not satisfactory for any real application. However, as we have seen, expanding the database is elementary.

A second improvement would be to add to the cleverness of the program. One way of generating an adjectival group which is synonymous with a given adjective is to cycle through the chain of opposites to that adjective and negate the adjective finally chosen. This means that the data would need two kinds of pointers—one for each item pointing to the next synonym in the chain and another pointing to a possible antonym (word of opposite meaning) which will itself have pointers to its own synonym chain and antonym. However, as before, it is not necessary to have a pointer to every antonym—only to one item in an antonym chain. As every item in a synonym chain should, strictly speaking, be antonymous to every item in a chain which contains one antonym only one pointer is needed each way between the chains.

In reality language is not quite this logical. There are very few words which mean exactly the same as other words, and relatively few words which are exactly opposite in meaning. However, human minds seem to have some data structure of this kind which allows them to flick rapidly between words which are related in all sorts of ways, yet which do not all have thousands of pointers to all the other items in the dictionary.

7.3 Semantic networks

Structures in human and computer memory which maintain a complex set of relations of meaning in this way are generally called 'semantic networks'. This is a term from cognitive psychology used to describe the many interrelations that human beings hold in their heads. A more familiar equivalent in computing terms is the relational database. In both cases the principle is the same. Not only does data point to other items in memory but different pointers represent different relationships.

It is common for such relational data to be structured in such a way that the position of a pointer within a database can tell you (or the program) not only which data items it is pointing to but also what kind of relation it represents. For example, we could construct a simple database in which each record consisted of three bytes. The first byte points to an actual string which is the English (or ASCII) equivalent of a word or phrase. The second byte points to another three-byte entry which is synonymous with the first. The third byte points to another three-byte entry which is antonymous to the entry. We then know that if we want to list all the antonyms of a particular phrase we can chain through every third byte until we return to the first entry, printing the string pointed to by the first byte of each three-byte entry.

Obviously each entry can consist of as many pointers as we want. Relational databases may contain more bytes representing relationships between data than the actual data themselves. The trick is to try to design a system of pointers which encodes the maximum amount of relational information yet requires the minimum amount of searching for recovering a particular piece of information. One trick that works in some circumstances, for example, is to make each pointer contain two pieces of information. One piece is the pointing address we have talked about and the other is the 'name' of the pointer. In this way the database can be irregular in structure, so that some items can have many pointers and others few. There will be no confusion between data and pointers because each is preceded by its 'naming' byte. In such a case the names used for such bytes can themselves be pointers to the type of name.

For example, suppose we had a database of 'birds, beasts and flowers'. It is a feature of such data that the names of some items also represent relations between other items. For example, one animal is called 'cat', and another is 'a member of the cat family'. If we have a pointer for the relationship 'member of the cat family', then its name would actually be a pointer to the data item 'cat'. Human memory is probably structured in such a way as part of the unclear dividing line between data and addresses.

7.4 Frames

Many methods of describing the memory networks have been proposed. None have been shown to be perfect but several have either been modelled using computers or have been incorporated in software of some kind.

One powerful approach which has yielded interesting results with data which has 'intuitive' rather than logical structure is that based on the notion of frames or scripts. A frame can be thought of as a database record with a number of fields. More loosely we can think of it as an 'activity' or an 'idea' which has several aspects or components. The frame is a general concept of some kind with a particular structure. Its structure is realized by the relationships between all the slots (fields, components) in the frame.

Suppose we think about the concept of movement. There are a large number of related concepts, most of which are represented by verbs or verb phrases, which fit into the concept of movement. There are notions like travelling, which may involve either a person travelling, or an object, or an animal, or some combination of items from this list. There are notions to do with propulsion, where one entity causes another to move. There is the notion of exchange, where one thing moves towards one place while another object moves in the opposite direction. Intuitively it seems that all these notions are interconnected but it is rather difficult to describe the interconnections in such a way that a computer program could process or 'understand' them.

But suppose we tried to break all these concepts down into their basic elements and tried to describe them all in terms of movement plus some other elementary or 'primitive' concepts. In doing this we are trying to find the basic features of the meaning of such words. We will look at other aspects of feature-based analysis when we examine the semantics of words and the elements of human personality.

Let us start with the central notion of 'motion'. This is the name of our frame. Now let us take just one simple verb and see what has to be involved for it to make sense. Put it another way—let us see what slots the motion frame has to have in order for a particular verb to fit into that frame. Let us start with 'walk'. Firstly someone has to do the walking. So we need an agent slot. The walker has to be walking from somewhere. Call this the origin. And he or she has to be going somewhere. Call this the destination. He/she has to travel by using a route and the route must connect origin and destination.

Compare this with the verb 'run'. Could we fit 'run' into a frame made up of agent, origin, destination and route? Yes, but there is a difference between 'walk' and 'run'. We need a slot for speed as well. Okay. How about a rather different verb, like 'ride'. The difference between 'ride' and 'walk' or 'run' is that a conveyance is involved.

What about 'take'? Well, this can fit except that an object is involved and the destination must be the location of the agent. Or, in plainer terms, if someone takes something they move it from its original location into the same location as themselves.

In fact we can describe a large category of verbs involving movement by using a frame which has the following categories:

AGENT—OBJECT—ROUTE—DIRECTION—SPEED—
ORIGIN—GOAL—CONVEYANCE—INSTRUMENT

Not only can we obtain something like a formal definition of a number of words (or idea) but, more importantly, we can do so in a way which relates several such ideas together. For example, we know that the verb 'give' is the opposite of 'take'. The only difference in their meanings is that in the former an object is moved away from the agent and towards another person, who is the recipient, whereas in the latter an object is moved towards the agent who is the recipient. So if we had a sentence like 'Joe gave the apple to Joanne', then a query like 'Who took the apple?' can be answered by reference to the relationships between the frames for the verbs 'take' and 'give'.

7.5 Conceptual dependency

The notion of patterns in language, or frames, has led to a second approach to parsing sentences. While this approach still relies to some extent on representing grammar in a form something like ATN grammars (as described in Chapter 5) it adds the additional information that syntactic structures are not purely syntactic. They are semantic as well and therefore in decoding the meaning of a given sentence we should pay attention to its semantic patterns as well as to its grammatical structure. For example, our discussion of frames has shown us that there is a close relationship between the meanings of 'give' and 'take'. Therefore if we have a program which is parsing a sentence containing such words it might gain valuable information about the overall meaning of the sentence by trying to fill the slots for the meaning of 'give' or 'take' rather than just looking at the syntactic categories of the words as held in the dictionary.

Although, as we saw, ATN grammars contain tree structures, recursive structures, searches for word categories, word forms and substructures, ultimately all the analysis conducted by such a parser is a series of consultations of a dictionary of syntactic forms. This can be unsatisfactory for a number of reasons. One is that, as we have seen when we considered memory, human information processing does not proceed all at one level. We do not simply process the words in a sentence, then its syntax and then its meaning; we do all these things in parallel. Furthermore we use information gleaned at one level to make decisions at another level. For example, if we encounter a spoken sentence such as 'Barking wildly the black dok attacked the postman' we will actually hear 'dog' rather than 'dok' because we have already gained a good idea of the meaning of the sentence from the semantic clues in 'barking'.

A further reason for wanting to improve on ATN grammars is the processing time that such an analysis can take. In an ATN grammar a program continues to pursue one line of analysis until it fails at some stage or another, i.e., a state is reached which is not the final state yet none of the transitions from it can be made. It then backs up to the previous level and tries to explore the next alternative transition. If all transitions at this level fail it backs up further and tries again. Thus in the worst possible case an

ATN grammar may try every possible case before it reaches its final parse. In many cases this can be avoided if information about the overall structure of the sentence was available to it. One way to provide such information is to conduct several parallel parses at different points in the structure rather than a straightforward left-to-right parse. However, this is very difficult to implement on serial processors.

A second approach is to work from the bottom upwards as well as from the top down, i.e., to try to construct noun groups wherever nouns occur, verb groups wherever verbs occur and so on, while also conducting a standard ATN parse. Information about the availability of, for example, noun groups when trying to construct a prepositional phrase thus helps to reduce the number of possible routes at any given stage in the parse. This is also difficult because it implies a degree of parallel processing and/or a way of switching between bottom-up and top-down parsing at appropriate moments in the analysis.

The third approach is to try and fit the sentence into some kind of frame. As nouns and verbs are the most important words in the language it seems sensible to spot these and then suggest a frame that might fit one of those identified keywords. The program then looks for the syntactic structures that would fit with that frame and ignores all other possible transitions. Providing the correct word is chosen as keyword and there is a suitable frame available, this process can not only substantially shorten processing time but can also greatly increase the apparent understanding of the system. The main drawbacks are the lack of suitable frames with clear enough specification for practical use and the complexity of the problems that can result if the program chooses the wrong keyword or tries to apply the wrong frame.

An example program is given as Fig. 7.2 which parses a sentence containing 'gave' or 'took'. Note that, unlike most of the programs in this book, this parser has no database. In other words it has no dictionary other than the fact that it expects one of two possible verbs. Therefore it cannot be using information about word forms or word types, or syntactic information held in a dictionary, to carry out its parse. And if it were it would need a very large dictionary, because it will parse just about any simple sentence you like providing one of the two keywords is used.

How does it work, then? Quite simply it uses some general rules about the likely position of syntactic units and how they relate to the meaning of the keyword. It knows that the subject usually comes before the verb, the object comes immediately after and the indirect object last. As it places all input words in an array in the order in which they are typed in it therefore can identify the verb by straightforward character by character comparison and

```
100 CLS
110 letter$=""
120 t$="*abcdefghijklmnopqrstuvwxyz " & CHR$(10)
130 DIM sentence$(w,l)
140 w=10
150 l=12
160 s=1
170 t=0
180 PRINT "Type a sentence using ´gave´ or ´took´"
190 AT 3,8:PRINT "[Only use lower case]"
200 REPeat store
210 word$=""
220 REPeat word
230 REPeat keyboard
240 letter$=INKEY$(0)
250 IF letter$="" THEN GO TO 240
260 IF letter$ INSTR t$ >1 THEN EXIT keyboard
270 END REPeat keyboard
280 AT 8,(t):PRINT letter$
290 t=t+1
300 IF letter$ <> " " AND letter$ <> CHR$(13) THEN word$ = word$ & letter$
310 IF letter$=" " OR  letter$=CHR$(10) THEN EXIT word
320 END REPeat word
330 sentence$(s)=word$
340 s=s+1
350 IF s=w OR letter$=CHR$(10) THEN EXIT store
360 END REPeat store
370 verb
380 IF verbflag<>1 THEN STOP
390 actor
400 direction
410 object
420 STOP
```
Figure 7.2 *(continues)*

```
430 :
440 DEFine PROCedure verb
450 verbflag=0
460 FOR i = 1 TO w
470 IF sentence$(i)="gave" OR sentence$(i)="took" THEN
480 PRINT "Verb is ";sentence$(i):v=i
490 verbflag=1
500 END IF
510 NEXT i
520 IF verbflag<>1 THEN PRINT "No verb"
530 END DEFine verb
540 :
550 DEFine PROCedure actor
560 PRINT "Actor is ";sentence$(v-1)
570 a=v-1
580 END DEFine actor
590 :
600 DEFine PROCedure direction
610 FOR i = 1 TO w
620 IF sentence$(i)="to" THEN
630 PRINT "Object goes to ";sentence$(art(i)):PRINT "Object goes from ";sentence$(a)
640 END IF
650 IF sentence$(i)="from" THEN
660 PRINT "Object goes from ";sentence$(art(i)):PRINT "Object goes to ";sentence$(a)
670 END IF
680 NEXT i
690 END DEFine direction
700 :
710 DEFine PROCedure object
720 o=art(v)
730 PRINT "Object is ";sentence$(o)
740 END DEFine object
750 :
760 DEFine FuNction art(x)
```
Figure 7.2 (*continues*)

```
770 IF sentence$(x+1)="the" OR
sentence$(x+1)="a" OR sentence$(x+1)="an"
THEN
780   RETurn x+2
790 ELSE
800   RETurn x+1
810 END IF
820 END DEFine art$
```

Figure 7.2

remember which array element holds that word. The subject is consequently the word held by the element immediately before the verb's and the object is the one immediately after it (unless there is an article, in which case it is the word after that). Finally it knows that the indirect object will be signalled by one of the prepositions 'to' or 'from'.

It is then a simple matter to assign the frame slots (or the necessary 'concepts') to each word. The subject is the actor, i.e., the person doing the giving or taking. The object being given is the syntactic object (the fact that the two words are identical is no coincidence). The remaining person is the recipient if in a 'to' phrase and the giver if in a 'from' phrase.

Of course it is easy to fool this program. Use a different tense of verb, make the expression passive, add adverbs before or after the verb, change the position of object and indirect object, and the program will fail. However, all of these difficulties can be overcome by allowing for alternatives by combining the conceptual model with an ATN model.

Even the difficulties such programs encounter when given the wrong keyword or ungrammatical sentences are being surmounted to some extent as programs are given strategies for 'best-guessing'. This highlights another defect of the ATN approach. Usually in an ATN grammar if the sentence is only slightly ungrammatical or if the grammar can almost make a satisfactory parse it nevertheless fails completely. As far as ATN descriptions go, either a sentence is grammatical or it is not. But by using frames (or, as it is sometimes called, the notion of 'conceptual dependency') if a partial interpretation can be arrived at the program may be able to achieve some results. It may, for example, 'guess' the missing information by filling in blank slots with default values it has. It may even assume that words or structures in the text that it has not been able to parse can be fitted into vacant slots if there is nowhere else for them to go.

For example, in a sentence like 'Sue give to Jack book', which is ungrammatical but typical of people learning English as a second language or of young children, the parser will be looking for an object which is being given, someone who is giving and someone who is receiving. 'Sue' looks like the giver because it is in the subject position. But is 'Jack' or 'book' the object, and who is the receiver? Our ATN parse would give up because the sentence does not fit any grammatical pattern. But the conceptual parse is looking for a 'to' phrase, an animate noun (recipient) and another noun, probably inanimate (object). It can find all of those even though they are not in their grammatical positions, so though it may be unhappy with the grammar it can still guess with a reasonable amount of certainty that 'Jack' is the recipient and 'book' is the object being given.

If the program in Fig. 7.2 were rewritten so that it first found the prepositional phrase and removed it from the array, then regarded any noun after the verb as the object, then even this simple illustrative program could cope with the problem by combining its syntactic analysis with its semantic.

The key point is not that this enables successful parsing of sentences but that the meanings underlying dozens of different sentences can all be related to each other in terms of a few basic frames and the slots within those frames. Decoding a particular text is then a question of finding the key idea (i.e., the frame) and then filling all the slots in the frame with suitable information in the text. Where no information on a particular slot is available the program can either request further information on that area ('Joe gave his book away'—Query: 'Who did Joe give the book to?') or can supply default information ('Joe gave the book away'—'to somebody else') or it can assume that the particular slot is not relevant to the current verb or text. (If Joe gave the book away and the speed of his action is not mentioned it is not important but if an adverb like 'quickly' occurs in the text put that in the speed slot.)

Using a system of frames will also allow complex manipulation and interpretation of data similar to that we have just examined in the synonym program. The relations between all verbs of movement can be regarded as a set of links represented by the slots they fill. For example, all verbs of movement must fill the 'object' slot. In the case of 'walk' the object being moved is the person doing the walking. In the case of 'kick' the object being moved is not the person doing the kicking, unless the pronoun 'himself' or 'herself' is used, e.g., 'Joe kicked himself'. There is always an agent of movement and there is always an object being moved which may or may not be the agent.

So it always makes sense to ask 'Who did the moving?' and 'What was moved?' Just as synonyms are connected by a slot called 'means the same as' so all verbs of movement are connected by the slots called 'agent' and 'object'.

However, only some verbs of movement use the speed slot or the conveyance slot. Conceptually speaking 'run' is the same as 'walk quickly', although we know that the actual movements are different. But there is no verb meaning 'give quickly'. There are verbs meaning 'take quickly' however, such as 'snatch' and 'grab'. The verbs 'take' and 'give' never fill the conveyance slot, however. So if we find a text like 'Joe took a train to Chicago' we know that the proper interpretation of this is not 'Joe appropriated a train' nor is it 'Joe took something (unnamed) using a train as a means of conveying that something.' We know it means that Joe rode a train because a conveyance and destination are mentioned but the verb 'to take' meaning 'to appropriate' always has the agent as its destination (and Chicago is not the agent, Joe is) and never fills the conveyance slot.

Naturally, reasoning like this seems almost absurd to human beings. But computers have the greatest difficulty over such matters. It is important that data structures are devised which are close to human thought processes if programmers are ever to produce programs which the majority of people will agree are, in some sense, intelligent. This is even more true if we want systems which are friendly to ordinary human beings. They must understand ordinary human beings. We will return to this topic when we look at ways of modelling personality.

7.6 Scripts

'Frames' were first developed by Marvin Minsky. Various people pursued various aspects of his work and a particularly interesting path of development was created by Schank and Abelson in their work on scripts. The difference between a frame and a script is quite simply that frames represent what might be called static information (words, ideas, concepts) just like a dictionary, but scripts represent a sequence of events or a narrative. We began to examine scripts when we considered story-writing programs in Chapter 4.

A script is just like a frame because it represents a chunk of human knowledge and sees that knowledge as made up of a series of slots which have to be filled for the script to be complete. Scripts differ from frames because they represent process over time, so different slots will have been filled at different moments in a particular decoding process.

The most commonly quoted script of Schank and Abelson is the restaurant script. They approach the problem by considering texts like: 'Joe was hungry so he went to Wimpy's. He ate two hamburgers but only had sixty pence so had to do the washing up.' This is a trivial, but typical, story. It is typical because all sorts of information that is needed for understanding the story is not supplied by it. A computer could not begin to process such a narrative because it simply could not find all the necessary information in the text.

For example, how does it know what 'Wimpy's' is? Why does only having 60 pence mean that Joe had to do the washing up? Where did the hamburgers come from? What has 60 pence to do with hamburgers? We know the answers to these questions but how could a computer?

Schank and Abelson say that human beings can answer such questions because they have a general model of such situations called, in this case, the restaurant script. The model contains such 'slots' as 'location—place where food is bought'; 'motivation—go to restaurant if hungry'; 'name—a restaurant has a name, usually a proper noun'; 'ordering—the customer must order food to obtain it' and so on. In fact we have an internalized script for a general story and when we hear a particular story like this we strive to make it fit the model.

So our internal story is something like: Joe is hungry. If you are hungry one of the things you can do is go to a restaurant. So Joe looked for a restaurant and found one. He then went there and ordered some food. He then ate the food. Having eaten the food he is expected to pay for it, which means he needs money. Two hamburgers are moderately expensive so 60 pence is probably not enough to pay for them. If you cannot pay in a restaurant you are usually punished in some way, often by being arrested or by being forced to wash up.

If a computer is given a general model of the usual sequence of events it can attempt to match up each section of a given text to one or more of the slots in its model. It will attempt to match each chunk of text to each slot in the order given in the model (e.g., you eat the food before you pay for it), and if it manages to match two chunks of text to two slots but has empty slots between them it will fill those empty slots with default values. A script is thus a sequence of default values for a sequence of events triggered by a keyword, such as 'hungry' or 'restaurant'. For example, in the text 'Joe wanted to buy a QL but he was hungry. So he went to Wimpy's then he bought his QL' the whole of the restaurant script is implied but none of the slots are filled except the 'go to restaurant' slot.

Incidentally there is also the additional script of 'buying a computer' which is only indicated here and we presumably understand all the appropriate stages in that script as well. We also understand that, for Joe at least, the goal 'satisfy hunger' (which is one of the restaurant slots) is more important than the goal 'get QL' because of the order in which the two scripts are called up. Arguably therefore these two scripts are themselves slots in a larger script which we might call the 'daily life' script, which is made up of such slots as 'waking up', 'getting dressed', 'satisfying hunger', 'satisfying other goals', 'resting' and so on. This must be the case because we do not imagine that Joe does nothing else in his day but eat a meal and buy a computer. It is simply that the rest of his day is implied or 'understood'. We know it because we have a model made up of a default sequence of events, and each of those slots itself is a model made up of other slots which themselves might be scripts of other kinds of events.

Naturally we do not follow the whole thing through to the greatest level of detail. Human beings are able to 'flick through' any given script and just to fill in the slots which are important in the current situation. Computers are not so lucky. The only way they can make a reasonable decision about the relevance of a piece of background information is to see if it helps solve another problem. However, the idea of scripts does provide a way of coping with this if we can design a hierarchy or tree of scripts such that a program only attempts to fill in slots at a particular level of specificity if it is necessary to solve a problem at a higher level of generality.

For example, a text might read 'Joe wanted to buy a QL but he was hungry. He went to Wimpy's. Sue came in. She said she had a QL to sell. Joe ate two hamburgers. He had three hundred pounds and sixty pence, so he gave Sue three hundred pounds and had to do the washing up.'

Here two scripts are combined. How can a computer (or, for that matter, a reader) decide what is going on? I think you will agree that the story line is quite clear. Joe goes to the restaurant because he is hungry. By chance he meets Sue who has the means to satisfy another of his goals. So he buys the QL, but this does not leave him enough money to pay for his food, so he has to do the washing up. We are presented with two general slots in the 'everyday life script': 'satisfy hunger' and 'satisfy subsidiary goals'. In order to fill the first we must call up (and fill some of the slots in) the restaurant script. In order to fill the second we must do the same for the buying a computer script.

But in order to understand why Joe had to do the washing up we have to see that a necessary part of the restaurant script is 'paying for food' and a necessary part of buying a computer is 'paying for computer'. Both of these can only be satisfied if the everyday life slot 'possessing money' is filled at the appropriate moment in each script. Early in the restaurant script the slot could be filled, because Joe had over three hundred pounds, but this is not the relevant moment for that slot to be filled. It is relevant only after the food has been eaten. But before this position in the restaurant script is reached the slot 'give money to person selling object' is filled in the 'buying a computer' script. This now means that the carrying money slot cannot be filled when it is needed in the restaurant script, so the 'punish nonpayer' slot is filled instead.

By creating models of the patterns within patterns, frames within frames and scripts within scripts in this way, the problem of context can gradually be overcome.

8 Meaning and learning

8.1 The need to learn

An intelligent person is able to learn. Most of the things that make sense in our world do so because of what we have learned about them rather than because of intrinsic properties in the things themselves. So our intelligent machine should also be able to learn. When we come to consider expert systems in Chapter 9 we will see how learning can be an important part of a practical system. For the moment let us just look at how a system might be made to learn in some fashion without wondering what use it might serve.

Human beings learn all sorts of different things in many different ways. But one of the easiest and most common ways of learning is by example. If we want to learn how to speak French we listen to other people speaking French and try to imitate them. If we want a child to behave 'properly' we try to behave in that way to teach the child by our own example. By hearing or seeing many examples, the learner of French or the child will produce some generalizations and use these as rules for how to act appropriately in future situations.

So if we wanted a computer to learn in the same way we could try giving it a number of examples of something and hope that it can sort out the general principles from the many examples. This method, called induction, is used by some expert systems, though they do not, generally, rely on hope. Instead they rely on forming hypotheses (in the form of one or more 'rules') which are tested against each example. If the test proves successful (i.e., the hypothesis seems to be correct) the rule is left alone, but for examples where the hypothesis fails the rule is altered slightly and then another example is taken.

In its simplest form such a learning process can be thought of as a series of questions and answers. If the computer knows that a given object has a number of features, then it can ask questions that test each feature. If all the features are found, then it can reasonably conclude that the object in question is the chosen object. If, however, one or more questions get a negative answer, then it can conclude that it is probably on the wrong track. This can also work with negative features. If the machine knows that a house is something that is lived in, an affirmative answer to the question 'Can someone live in the object?' suggests that it is a house. If it knows that houses do not have legs then a negative answer to the question 'Does it have legs?' could also be regarded as a positive indication that the object in question might be a house.

However, both positive and negative responses can seldom be certain indications. One question on its own is seldom enough to identify an object for certain. This is because most objects have a number of properties and to learn the full 'meaning' of any given object (or, to put it differently, a word referring to any object) means understanding that the object has many qualities, may have others, lacks others and is like many other kinds of object.

By using what is called a 'feature-based' description of objects we can go some way to defining them in such a way that a computer can understand them and therefore learn about them. For example, if we took the features 'young', 'old', 'male' and 'female' we could do the following analysis of the words 'man', 'woman', 'boy' and 'girl'.

WORD	YOUNG	OLD	MALE	FEMALE
MAN	−	+	+	−
WOMAN	−	+	−	+
BOY	+	−	+	−
GIRL	+	−	−	+

In this way we have defined the four terms so that knowledge of just two features can tell us which word is meant. As such an analysis is essentially binary we can reduce the number of terms, because something that is male cannot be female and something that is young cannot be old. We actually need only two features, old and male. A girl would thus be defined as [−old −male], a man as [+old +male]. Providing you choose the right features many areas of knowledge can be represented in this way. Once such information is reduced to binary then it can be handled by a computer and it can be used as the basis of actions or 'conclusions'.

8.2 Making comparisons

For example, take the complicated business of deciding whether two words mean the same thing, similar things or different things. There are many different kinds of relations between things and between words which feature-based analysis can reduce to simpler relationships. If we wanted a program which could produce similes and contradictions in order to provide creative ideas for our latest work of modern literature we could build a feature-based dictionary of possible words and write a program which could compare any two items in terms of those features.

An example is given here for you to expand as you desire. The program contains semantic information on 22 words commonly used in English similes and comparisons. They are all nouns and therefore can be thought of as definitions of objects. The features used to define these words cover colour, weight, hardness, strength and heat so that traditional comparisons like 'as heavy as lead' and 'as black as soot' would be contained within this data. Information on the objects is coded as in Fig. 8.1.

Each feature is marked 1 if present and 0 if absent. Although you might think that we could reduce a binary pair like 'hot/cold' to a single either/or (1 or 0) we cannot because for some words and objects the temperature is irrelevant and coding the feature in either way will lead to mistakes in processing it. For example, if we thought that 'rose' was not hot, therefore should be cold, we would be likely to get expressions like 'as cold as a rose' which, though it might mean something to someone, could hardly be called proverbial or a particularly apt comparison. We only mark those features which are present but do not regard absence of a feature as signifying presence of its opposite. You will see that they have been arranged as one set of seven and one set of eight, so can be coded as a pair of bytes. The decimal representation of each set of features is given in two columns on the right of the table and these are held in the data statements in the program (Fig. 8.2) next to the relevant words.

The program gives the user two choices. It will produce either a comparison or a potential contradiction as selected by the user. For a comparison it simply finds two words which have the same feature and reports the basis of the comparison. For a contradiction it chooses between two approaches depending on whether the contradiction is in terms of colour or the other features. For colour we have to find two words with different features in the colour byte; for the other features it is necessary to find two adjacent bits of which one is set in each word and the other is reset.

Any semantic analysis can be based on such features. For example, in an adventure game all the characters could be given personal characteristics in the same way as objects have physical characteristics. Or if we are trying to parse a sentence we can use the semantic information as part of the grammatical analysis. In the creative programs we have already looked at, a feature-based description of the words used makes generation of meaningful text or useful ideas more likely.

	B R I G H T	W H I T E	Y E L L O W	G R E E N	B L U E	R E D	B L A C K	H O T	C O L D	S T R O N G	W E A K	H A R D	S O F T	H E A V Y	L I G H T		
snow	0	0	1	0	0	0	0	0	1	0	0	0	0	1	0	32	69
iron	0	0	0	0	0	0	1	1	1	0	0	0	1	0	1	1	74
coal	0	0	0	0	0	0	1	0	1	0	0	0	0	0	0	8	8
grass	0	0	0	1	0	0	0	0	0	0	0	0	0	0	0	4	4
sky	0	0	0	0	1	0	0	0	1	0	0	0	0	1	1	0	1
silk	0	0	0	0	0	0	0	1	0	1	0	0	1	0	0	0	5
tea	0	0	0	0	0	1	0	0	1	0	0	0	0	0	1	8	5
cucumber	0	0	0	1	0	0	0	0	0	0	0	0	0	0	0	2	64
cherry	0	0	0	0	0	1	0	0	0	0	0	0	0	0	0	1	0
lead	0	0	0	0	0	0	0	0	1	0	0	0	0	0	0	1	6
soot	0	0	0	0	0	0	1	1	1	0	0	0	0	0	0	2	5
fire	0	0	0	0	0	1	0	1	0	1	0	0	0	1	0	1	1 28
oxen	0	1	0	0	0	0	1	0	0	1	0	0	0	1	0	2	34
steel	0	0	0	0	0	0	0	1	1	0	0	0	1	0	0	96	1 0 6
gold	0	0	1	0	0	0	0	0	0	0	0	1	0	0	0	1 6	2
ice	0	0	0	0	0	0	0	0	0	0	1	1	0	0	1	32	72
feather	0	0	1	0	0	0	0	0	0	0	0	0	0	0	0	32	5
water	0	1	0	0	0	0	0	0	0	1	0	0	0	1	0	64	80
diamond	0	1	0	0	0	0	0	0	0	0	0	0	0	1	0	64	72
man	0	0	0	0	0	0	0	0	0	0	0	0	1	1	0	0	60
rose	0	0	0	0	0	1	0	0	0	0	0	0	0	0	0	2	4
berry	0	1	0	0	0	1	0	0	0	0	0	0	0	0	0	66	0

Figure 8.1

```
100 init
110 REPeat control
120 CLS
130 PRINT\ "Comparison (1) or contradiction (2)?"
140 REPeat getloop
150 choice$=INKEY$:IF choice$=""THEN GO TO 150
160 IF choice$="1" OR choice$="2" THEN EXIT getloop
170 END REPeat getloop
180 c=CODE(choice$)
190 SELect ON c
200 =49:compare
210 =50:contradict
220 END SELect
230 AT 18,11:PRINT "Again (Y/N)?"
240 REPeat getloop
250 yn$=INKEY$
260 IF yn$=""THEN GO TO 250
270 yn= yn$ INSTR "YyNn"
280 IF yn<>0 THEN EXIT getloop
290 END REPeat getloop
300 IF yn>2 THEN EXIT control
310 END REPeat control
320 STOP
330 :
340 :
350 DEFine PROCedure init
360 RESTORE
370 name_no=22
380 prop_no=15
390 DIM name$(name_no,20),colour(name_no),qual(name_no),property$(prop_no,20)
400 FOR i = 1 TO name_no
410 READ name$(i)
420 READ colour(i)
```

Figure 8.2 *(continues)*

```
430 READ qual(i)
440 NEXT i
450 FOR i= 1 TO prop_no
460 READ property$(i)
470 NEXT i
480 END DEFine init
490 :
500 :
510 DEFine PROCedure compare
520 r=RND(1 TO name_no)
530 REPeat bloop
540 s=RND(1 TO 22)
550 colread=colour(r) && colour(s)
560 qualread=qual(r) && qual(s)
570 IF (colread<>0 OR qualread<>0) AND r<>s THEN EXIT bloop
580 END REPeat bloop
590 STRIP 7:INK 0
600 AT 6,6:PRINT name$(r);" is like ";name$(s)
610 STRIP 2:INK 7
620 PRINT\\"(Because they are both ";
630 IF colread>0 THEN colprint
640 IF colread>0 AND qualread>0 THEN PRINT;" and ";
650 IF qualread>0 THEN qualprint
660 PRINT")"
670 END DEFine compare
680 :
690 :
700 DEFine PROCedure contradict
710 t=RND(1 TO 2)
720 SELect ON t
730 =1:contracol
740 =2:contraqual
750 END SELect
760 END DEFine contradict
770 :
```

Figure 8.2 (*continues*)

```
780 :
790 DEFine PROCedure contracol
800 REPeat cloop
810 r=RND(1 TO name_no)
820 s=RND(1 TO name_no)
830 colread=(colour(r)    colour(s))
840 IF colread<>0 AND colour(r)<>0 AND colour(s)<>0 AND s<>r THEN EXIT cloop
850 END REPeat cloop
860 AT 5,4:STRIP 7:INK 0:PRINT "The ";name$(r);" is like the ";name$(s):STRIP 2:INK 7
870 PRINT\\"could be a contradiction because they are different colours"
880 END DEFine contracol
890 :
900 :
910 DEFine PROCedure contraqual
920 r=RND(1 TO name_no)
930 REPeat dloop
940 s=RND(1 TO name_no)
950 FOR i=0 TO 6 STEP 2
960 qualr=0
970 quals=0
980 IF (qual(r) && (2^i)) ^^ (qual(s) && (2^i)) THEN qualr=i
990 IF (qual(r) && (2^(i+1))) ^^ (qual(s) && (2^(i+1))) THEN quals=i+1
1000 IF qualr<>0 AND quals<>0 THEN EXIT dloop
1010 NEXT i
1020 END REPeat dloop
1030 STRIP 7:INK 0
1040 AT 4,4:PRINT "The ";name$(r);" is like the ";name$(s)
1050 STRIP 2:INK 7
1060 PRINT\\ "could be a contradiiction because one is ";property$(qualr+1)!" but one is ";property$(quals+1)
```

Figure 8.2 *(continues)*

```
1070 END DEFine contraqual
1080 :
1090 :
1100 DEFine PROCedure colprint
1110 vrec=0
1120 vnow=0
1130 FOR i = 0 TO 6
1140 IF colread && (2^i) THEN
1150 IF vnow> vrec THEN PRINT " and ";:vrec=vnow
1160 PRINT property$(9+i);
1170 vnow=vnow+1
1180 END IF
1190 NEXT i
1200 END DEFine colprint
1210 :
1220 :
1230 DEFine PROCedure qualprint
1240 FOR i = 0 TO 7
1250 vrec=0
1260 vnow=0
1270 FOR i = 0 TO 7
1280 IF qualread && (2^i) THEN
1290 IF vnow > vrec THEN PRINT " and ";:vrec=vnow
1300 PRINT property$(1+i);
1310 vnow=vnow+1
1320 END IF
1330 NEXT i
1340 END DEFine qualprint
1350 :
1360 :
1370 DATA "snow",32,69
1380 DATA "iron",1,74
1390 DATA "coal",1,8
1400 DATA "grass",8,4
1410 DATA "sky",4,1
1420 DATA "tea",0,144
```

Figure 8.2 (*continues*)

```
1430 DATA "silk",0,5
1440 DATA "cucumber",8,64
1450 DATA "cherry",2,0
1460 DATA "lead",1,6
1470 DATA "soot",1,5
1480 DATA "fire",2,128
1490 DATA "oxen",1,34
1500 DATA "steel",32,106
1510 DATA "gold",16,2
1520 DATA "ice",32,72
1530 DATA "feather",32,5
1540 DATA "water",0,80
1550 DATA "diamond",0,72
1560 DATA "man",0,60
1570 DATA "rose",2,4
1580 DATA "berry",2,0
1590 DATA
"light","heavy","soft","hard","weak","stron
g","cold","hot"
1600 DATA
"black","red","blue","green","yellow","whit
e","bright"
```
Figure 8.2

In each case, however, the usefulness of such an approach depends upon the features you have chosen to encode and the program which interprets the features. There would be little point in writing a program designed to analyse financial reports if the only encoded features were concerned with plants and fruits. Nor would a program using the data we have provided be very useful if it tried to relate the colour features to any of the other features.

8.3 How does the program work?

As usual the program contains a database which it acts on to produce its comparisons and contradictions. Procedure init is used to dimension the necessary arrays to hold the words (name$), the colour code for each word (colour), the quality or property code for each word (qual) and the names of all the properties (property$). These are dimensioned using the two declared variables name__no, which holds the number of words in the dictionary, and prop__no, which holds the number of properties that can be looked for. As in other programs this is to facilitate adaptation of the program if you wish to expand the database. Once declared the data held in lines 1370 to 1600 is read in.

The main loop, called control, which executes lines 110 to 310, has three stages. Firstly it asks the user if a comparison or a contradiction is to be generated. Secondly it uses the SELect . . . ON . . . statement to send control to either the comparison or the contradiction routines. IF . . . THEN . . . ELSE . . . could have been used to the same effect, but ON SELect allows you to add other relationships if you so wish without a great deal of rewriting of the control loop.

Having executed the choice lines 230 to 300, determine if the user wants to produce further input or to end the program.

There are only two main procedures in the program, though these use others. Procedure compare generates the comparisons. Firstly it chooses r, a random number to represent a word in the dictionary. It then generates a second random number, s, which is to be the second word. However, because word s may not compare with word r, the second random number must be produced in a repeat loop which continues until a number which does compare has been found. The exit condition for the loop called bloop is line 570, which can be interpreted as 'if there is a match between the colours of the two chosen words or there is a match between the properties of the two words, and the two words are not the same, then a suitable comparison has been found'.

The procedure recognizes that two words have the same property or colour by doing a bitwise comparison using the bitwise 'AND' function of Super-BASIC. This is represented by the sign &&. Bitwise AND compares two bytes. If any bit in both bytes is set, then that bit remains set. All other bits are reset to zero (i.e., if a bit is set in only one of the two bytes, or it is not set in either byte, it is reset). This results in a new byte which is made up of all bits which are set in both bytes. As we have coded our data as a bit pattern, the && function results in zero if any two words have no feature in common and some other value if they have features in common.

For example, 'rose' is soft. 'Snow' is also soft. The value for rose is 4, meaning bit 2 is set. The value for snow is 69, meaning bits 6, 2 and 1 are set. Bitwise 'AND' applied to these two numbers returns '4' because only bit 2 is set in both numbers. If you type in in immediate mode PRINT 69 && 4 you will get 4 as a result.

The comparisons are done in lines 550 and 560 with the resulting values being stored in colread and qualread.

When a suitable pair of words has been found, line 600 creates a strip of black ink on white paper to print out the two words. This is easy because the words are numbers r and s in the array name$. Less easy is explaining the grounds for the comparison. It may be one colour, several colours, one property, several properties, or some combination of these. This problem can be broken down into two stages:

1. Is the comparison on grounds of colour and/or property?
2. How many such comparisons are there?

Line 630 tests for colour as a ground of comparison and calls procedure colprint if there is a colour similarity. Line 650 does the same thing for property, calling procedure qualprint. Between them line 640 tests to see if both kinds of comparison can be made, printing an 'and' if they can.

Both colprint and qualprint effectively do the same thing. They use && to find which bits are set in the relevant variable (colread or qualread) and when they find a bit which is set they print out the name of the property coded by that bit.

Procedure contradict is slightly more complicated because we have to ensure that two words are different in some respect and remember what that difference is. Line 710 assigns a random value to t, which is then used as a control variable in the SELect ... ON ... statement in the next line. Unfortunately SuperBASIC does not allow the use of functions in the SELect statement so we cannot, for example, write SELect ON (RND(1 TO 2)). This is the choice of which area to search for the contradiction.

If contracol is selected, then an opposition of colours is looked for. Two random words, r and s, are selected and bitwise XOR (exclusive OR) is used to determined if they have different colours. SuperBASIC represents bitwise XOR as ^ ^. Its function is to compare two bytes and return a byte containing bits which are set if the corresponding bit in either byte was set, but not if both were set. In other words a bit is set if it is set in either but not both of the compared bytes. As any two words with the same colours have the same bits set this function returns 0, and so another pair of words has to be chosen.

Then, as with the comparison, a coloured strip is used to print out the chosen words.

Contraqual is more complex still, because we must make sure not only that the objects have different properties but that they have conflicting or opposite properties. As we have arranged the coding so that bits with opposite coding are next to each other, the routine has to find two words which have adjacent property bits set, where the lowest bit is an even-numbered bit or the zero bit. This last condition is necessary because we could find adjacent bits which are unrelated. For example 'cold' is next to 'strong', so simply looking for words with adjacent bits set could result in a cold word being regarded as opposite to a strong word.

First the procedure chooses a word. Then it chooses a second word and cycles through all the bits of both words, looking at pairs of bits. If it finds any pair for which one word has one bit set and the other word has the other bit, then it returns the bit numbers to qualr and quals. Two tests are needed to do this. One tests that bit i is set for only one of the words and the other tests that bit i + 1 is set for only one of the words. These tests, in line 980 and 990, are othewise the same.

Both take the current bit, which is the variable i controlling the FOR ... NEXT loop or i + 1, and find the value of 2^i. This is the decimal value of the given bit. This is then compared with the byte for the one word using &&. If this bit is set in the word, then it will return a byte with just that bit set, otherwise 0. The same test is applied to the other chosen word. This gives two bytes, one or both of which may have the given bit set. Thus if we now compare these two bytes using ^^ we will get a non-zero result only if one of the two bytes has the bit set. This therefore tells us that one, and only one, of the words has that bit set.

If this test is applied to both adjacent bits, then if both times a non-zero result is given we know that both bits are set for only one of the words. The only problem would arise if both bits could be set for one word and neither for the other. Although this is logically possible of course, it cannot happen with the data we are using because adjacent bits are mutually exclusive. No word will be both hot and cold, for example.

The remainder of contraqual prints the words and the qualities in the same way as the other two main procedures we have examined.

8.4 A deductive machine

In Chapter 9 we will examine programs that carry out deduction largely with help from the user. They have to interrogate the user and obtain information from him or her in order to learn about a situation and hence arrive at a conclusion. For the moment let us consider a program that could use a different approach. Instead of going through each stage of the deductive process one stage at a time and asking for additional information each time there is a binary decision to make, it could take in more than one piece of information to start with and attempt to derive conclusions from that information.

This means that the program has to be able to search for a number of possible semantic relationships and must be able to carry out chains of reasoning without aid from the user. The comparison program earlier in this chapter does elementary semantic analysis but only at one level of deduction. Reasoning, however, involves many stages of analysis, and each must be carried out correctly with all available information.

This brings us to one of the main difficulties faced by researchers in AI. If you are to go through a number of stages of analysis searching even small amounts of data there, you will almost certainly face the problem of 'combinatorial explosion'. Suppose you have forty items of data each with ten possible features and your search procedure involves four stages of reasoning. You might therefore have to compare 40 items × 10 features to find the first stage of the deduction, × (40 × 10) for the second, × (40 × 10) for the third, giving a total of 64 000 000 operations before you can be certain of finding the correct conclusion!

So severe can this problem become that the infamous Lighthill report of 1973 claimed that AI would never have any major success because of this problem and effectively prevented any major funding being given to AI research in Britain for many years. However, efficient search routines can reduce this substantially, and other techniques can be used to replace methods which require complete and blind search. One method is to try to estimate the most likely areas of the data which are worth searching most thoroughly, another is to put some form of time limit on the search related to the potential value of that particular aspect of the search. These, and other methods designed to combat the problem of combinatorial explosion, are further examples of the 'heuristics' we have already briefly encountered.

One method of reasoning is called 'backward chaining'. This is a process whereby you start your search not from the information provided as data but from the desired conclusion. Then you try to determine what is the best state immediately before that conclusion, then the one before that, then the one before that until you end up with a state that corresponds to your starting position. For example, if Charles wants to persuade Bessie to give him a birthday present Charles might decide that Bessie must be told about his birthday in order to do this. So Charles has to find some way of letting Bessie know it's his birthday. Perhaps Charles decides that Alf should be persuaded to tell Bessie. So Charles needs some way of persuading Alf. So he might decide to ask Alf when Bessie's birthday is, as a way of introducing the topic.

So he has to contact Alf. And so on, until Charles gets back to the point he is currently at, sitting in his armchair thinking 'How can I get Bessie to buy me that IBM?'

Let us finish this examination of reasoning processes by creating a program which can make deductions. It uses no complex search techniques but can perform long chains of logical reasoning. Essentially it works by a process called syllogistic reasoning. A syllogism is a series of logical statements whereby a conclusion can be validly reached from a given premise (in other words, forward chaining, relying entirely on logic). An example of a simple syllogism is:

1. An orange is a fruit.
2. All fruit is edible.
3. Therefore an orange is edible.

The logic says: '*A* is *B*, *B* is *C*, so *A* is *C*.' Returning to our comparison program we can say that it contains some elementary syllogisms, such as:

1. Snow is cold.
2. Ice is cold.
3. Therefore snow is like ice.

However, the program below is a little more intelligent because it allows long chains of logic and it allows the user to define the information from which conclusions are to be drawn. Thus the program is dependent on truthful (or at least meaningful) statements being given to it in the first place, but when they are it can answer questions about the data, relationships between the data and the inferences which can be derived from that data and the relationships within them.

8.5 The syllogism program

The aim of the program (Fig. 8.3) is to find logical relations between English statements. It therefore allows only two kinds of input, statements which are true and questions about the items in those statements. The program therefore requires an input routine which parses the input and decides whether it is a statement or a question, and two major components which are called depending which of the two forms of input are used. In this respect, therefore, the program is a simple example of the application of a grammar as suggested in Chapter 5. However, the grammar used here is much simpler than the ATN model given in that chapter, for it simply divides sentences into noun phrases and a relationship between such phrases.

```
100 number=0
110 CLS
120 init
130 instruct
140 REPeat in_loop
150 split=0
160 rel=0
170 qflag=0
180 n1$=""
190 n2$=""
200 PRINT
210 INPUT command$
220 PRINT
230 FOR i=1 TO LEN(command$)
240 IF CODE(command$(i))>96 THEN command$(i)=CHR$(CODE(command$(i))-32)
250 NEXT i
260 command$=" " & command$
270 IF "QUIT" INSTR command$ THEN EXIT in_loop
280 IF "IS " INSTR command$<3 THEN qflag=1
290 remove " IS "
300 IF command$(LEN(command$))="?" THEN
310 qflag=1
320 command$=command$(1 TO LEN(command$)-1)
330 END IF
340 IF command$(1)=" " THEN command$=command$(2 TO LEN(command$))
350 space= " " INSTR command$
360 temp$=command$(space TO LEN(command$))
370 artpos=0
380 artlen=0
390 findart(temp$)
400 n1$=" " & command$(1 TO space+artpos-2)
410 n2$=temp$(artpos+artlen TO LEN(temp$))
420 artpos=0
430 findart(n1$)
440 IF artpos>0 THEN n1$=n1$(artpos+artlen
```

Figure 8.3 *(continues)*

```
         TO LEN(nl$))
450 SELect ON qflag
460 =0:fact
470 =1:query
480 END SELect
490 END REPeat in_loop
500 STOP
510 :
520 DEFine PROCedure fact
530 insert nl$
540 nlpos=number
550 insert n2$
560 n2pos=number
570 alter nlpos,n2pos
580 END DEFine fact
590 :
600 DEFine PROCedure insert(n$)
610 i=0
620 REPeat loop
630 IF noun$(i)="" THEN
640 noun$(i)=n$
650 number=i
660 EXIT loop
670 END IF
680 IF noun$(i)=n$ THEN
690 number=i
700 EXIT loop
710 END IF
720 i=i+1
730 END REPeat loop
740 END DEFine insert
750 :
760 DEFine PROCedure alter(a,B)
770 item%(a,B)=1
780 REMark item%(B,a)=1
790 item%(a,a)=1
800 item%(B,B)=1
810 END DEFine alter
```

Figure 8.3 (*continues*)

```
820 :
830 DEFine PROCedure remove (st$)
840 LOCal x
850 REPeat loop
860 x=0
870 x= st$ INSTR command$
880 IF x=0 THEN EXIT loop
890 command$=command$(1 TO x-1)&
command$(x+LEN(st$)-1 TO LEN(command$))
900 IF command$(1)=" " THEN
command$=command$(2 TO LEN(command$))
910 IF x>split THEN split=x
920 END REPeat loop
930 RETurn
940 END DEFine remove
950 :
960 DEFine PROCedure query
970 LOCal x
980 LOCal y
990 x=0
1000 x=findpos(nl$)
1010 IF x=-1 THEN
1020 PRINT "I have no information on
´";nl$;"´"
1030 RETurn
1040 END IF
1050 y=0
1060 y=findpos(n2$)
1070 IF y=-1 THEN
1080 PRINT "I don´t have any information on
´";n2$;"´"
1090 RETurn
1100 END IF
1110 top=x
1120 bottom=y
1130 flag=0
1140 FOR i=0 TO 50
1150 used(i)=0
```

Figure 8.3 (*continues*)

```
1160 NEXT i
1170 finditem(top)
1180 IF flag=1 THEN
1190 PRINT "Yes"
1200 ELSE
1210 PRINT "Not according to my
information"
1220 END IF
1230 END DEFine query
1240 :
1250 DEFine PROCedure finditem(a)
1260 LOCal x
1270 LOCal i
1280 i=0
1290 IF a=low THEN flag=1
1300 IF flag=1 THEN RETurn
1310 REPeat gloop
1320 IF item%(a,i)=1 AND a<>i AND
used(i)<>1 THEN
1330 used(i)=1
1340 finditem(i)
1350 END IF
1360 IF i=50 OR flag=1 THEN EXIT gloop
1370 i=i+1
1380 END REPeat gloop
1390 END DEFine finditem
1400 :
1410 DEFine FuNction findpos(a$)
1420 LOCal z
1430 z=0
1440 REPeat floop
1450 IF noun$(z)=a$ THEN
1460 RETurn z
1470 EXIT floop
1480 END IF
1490 IF' noun$(z)="" THEN
1500 RETurn -1
1510 EXIT floop
```

Figure 8.3 (*continues*)

```
1520 END IF
1530 z=z+1
1540 END REPeat floop
1550 END DEFine findpos
1560 :
1570 DEFine PROCedure instruct
1580 PRINT \\"        TYPE A FACT OR A QUESTION"
1590 PRINT \"        FACTS MUST BE OF THE FORM:"
1600 STRIP 6
1610 INK 0
1620 AT 6,4:PRINT "<Noun Phrase> <IS> <Noun Phrase>"
1630 STRIP 2
1640 INK 7
1650 PRINT \"        QUESTIONS OF THE FORM:"
1660 STRIP 6
1670 INK 0
1680 AT 11,1:PRINT "<IS> <Noun Phrase> <Noun Phrase> <?>"
1690 STRIP 2
1700 INK 7
1710 PRINT\\" The second noun phrase must begin"!" with ´A´, ´AN´ or ´THE´ but these"!"    are optional for the first."
1720 PRINT\\"     [Press any key to continue]"
1730 g$=INKEY$:IF g$="" THEN GO TO 1730
1740 CLS
1750 END DEFine instruct
1760 :
1770 DEFine PROCedure init
1780 DIM noun$(50,20)
1790 DIM item%(50,50)
1800 DIM used(50)
1810 rel=0
```

Figure 8.3 (*continues*)

```
1820 END DEFine init
1830 :
1840 DEFine PROCedure findart(x$)
1850 artpos= " THE " INSTR x$:artlen=5
1860 IF artpos>0 THEN RETurn
1870 artpos= " A " INSTR x$:artlen=3
1880 IF artpos>0 THEN RETurn
1890 artpos= " AN " INSTR x$:artlen=4
1900 END DEFine findart
```
Figure 8.3

Most of the declaration of variables is done in the opening lines of the program, with procedure init simply dimensioning the main arrays. Noun$ is to hold the noun phrases, which may be single words or several words in length. Fifty characters are assigned for each phrase. No array is used to store the relations because only two are possible: x is a y and x is not a y. The array item% is used to hold a record of the relationship between different noun phrases and used is used temporarily to mark elements which have been searched during the decoding procedure.

At line 210 a sentence is input. Lines 230 to 250 ensure that the input string (command$) is all in upper case. A space is added to the beginning of command$ in line 260 so that all words in the sentence begin with spaces. This is to ensure that the test for 'IS' can apply anywhere in the input string. Line 270 checks for the word 'QUIT'. If it is somewhere in the input, then the program ends. (There is thus a slight flaw in the program as no statements or queries can use 'QUIT' as a substring.)

Lines 280 to 290 then find the position of the word 'IS' (which has to be bracketed by spaces to ensure that words like 'THIS' and 'MISS' are not treated as 'IS'. If the position of 'IS' is early in the string, command$ is treated as a question by setting qflag to 1. A second test at line 300 looks for a '?', which is also a marker of a question. In both cases 'IS' and '?' are removed so that the remaining routines can deal with the rest of the string.

Lines 350 to 440 then attempt to divide the rest of the string into two components, each of which will be regarded as a noun phrase. Line 360 skips the first word and stores the remainder in temp$. Line 390 then calls the function findart which attempts to find an article ('THE', 'A' or 'AN') in temp$. The position of the article is taken as the beginning of the second noun phrase. The first noun phrase is therefore everything up to that point.

These two substrings are stored as n1$ and n2$ in lines 400 and 410. Line 430 then calls findart again to discover the position of any article in n1$. If there is an article this is taken as the marker of the beginning of the noun phrase and n1$ is shortened accordingly. This means that the first noun phrase does not need an article but the second must have one.

Having identified the two noun phrases, either the procedure fact or the procedure query is called, depending on whether qflag has previously been set or not. The rest of the program is controlled by these two procedures.

Procedure fact simply places the new noun phrases in the list of noun phrases and adds a flag for their identity relationship to the array item%. It does this by calling the procedure insert twice, once with the first noun phrase as its parameter and the second time with the second noun phrase. Naturally we do not want to put any phrase in the list if it is already there, so procedure insert operates a loop which continues until it either finds an empty slot in noun$ or finds a string in noun$ which matches the target string.

If it finds an empty slot, then the target string is written to that slot and variable number remembers the number of the slot. If it finds a match, the phrase is not written in, but the element is still remembered in number. The value of number is passed back to the calling routine, where it is transferred either to n1pos or n2pos. When both phrases have been treated in this way we will thus have two variables, n1pos and n2pos, which hold the numbers of the elements in which those phrases reside. Procedure alter is therefore called with these two values as its parameters. Alter simply places the value 1 in the matrix item% at slots which correspond to the two phrase positions. Each row in item% represents an element in noun$ and each column in item% represents an element in noun$. At all the points where row and column for the values n1pos and n2pos intersect, the value 1 is placed. Thus where the column representing n1pos meets the row representing n1pos a 1 is placed, where the column representing n2pos meets the row representing n2pos a 1 is placed, where the column representing n1pos meets the row representing n2pos a 1 is placed and where the row representing n1pos meets the column representing n2pos a 1 is placed. (Or it would be if the REM were removed from line 780—but more of this anon.)

Procedure query first has to establish if the two phrases n1$ and n2$ are in its data. It does this by two calls to procedure findpos, which cycles through array noun$ until either it finds a match for the given string or it reaches an empty element in the array, which means it has been unable to find the target string. The value -1 is returned if the string is not found, otherwise the number of the element which holds the target string is returned. If -1 is returned, an error message is printed and control returned to the main loop.

However, if both phrases are in the database, then the program can carry out its inference procedure, which is to establish one thing. Is there a legitimate 'is a' relation between those two phrases? In the case of two phrases where the answer to the question was given as a statement (such as 'Fred is a fisherman'—'Is Fred a fisherman?') the program simply needs to look at the intersection of the two values for the phrases, i.e. the entry in item% which represents the column for 'Fred' and the row for 'a fisherman'. If that intersection is a 1, then the answer to the question is 'yes'.

But if the intersection is not 1 the answer is not necessarily 'no'. This would mean that no statement 'Fred is a fisherman' had been typed in. But what if the statements 'Fred is an angler' and 'An angler is a fisherman' had been given? Human logic tells us that this means Fred is a fisherman, so the answer should be 'yes'. How can the program discover this? If it looks at the intersection of 'Fred' and 'an angler' it finds a 1. If it looks at the intersection of 'an angler' and 'a fisherman' it finds a 1. So if it looks at all the entries for column 'Fred' until it found a 1, then looked at the column representing the element whose row intersected with column 'Fred' to give that 1 until it found a 1, then looked at the column for the row that intersected to give that 1 ... and so on, it would be tracing the patterns of interconnection. Every time a legitimate connection of column and row is found the routine begins to examine the column for that intersecting row. So if 'Fred' intersects with 'an angler' it will first look at column 'Fred' until it finds the intersection with row 'an angler'. It then examines row 'an angler' until it finds another intersection which, in our example, is 'a fisherman'. As 'a fisherman' is the target, it has succeeded, so can set a flag to 1 and end the search.

If, however, it could not find the target connection, how would it know when to stop? This must be when it has reached the first entry in the table, which means it must start searching at the lowest of the two entries (was 'Fred' or 'a fisherman' typed in last?) and work upwards through the table until it finds either the target element or the earliest element. We must also ensure that it does not get caught in the perpetual loop of finding a connection between a column and a row, then between the row for that column and the column for that row (e.g., 'an angler is a fisherman and a fisherman is an angler') because it would just keep going round and round in circles, so we use the array used to record each connection that has been found and pursued.

Procedure finditem is therefore a recursive procedure. Firstly it declares two local variables x and i. These will be 'new' variables each time the procedure is called, even if it calls itself. They are local to the procedure they are declared in and cannot be used by any other procedure. Variable a, which holds the value of the element at the top of the table (i.e., the phrase of the two we are searching for which is the newest entry, at the top of the table). Variable low is the value for the other element we are looking for, the one which is oldest or lowest in the table and towards which we are proceeding. Line 1290 therefore tests to see if a is equal to low. If it is, then the element being looked for has been found, but this test always fails when the procedure is first called because a and low are not the same unless a question like 'Is an angler an angler?' has been asked.

The loop 1310 to 1380 does the searching. It looks at column a, examining each row in turn (represented by the constantly incremented variable i). At line 1320, if item%(a,i)=1 (i.e., the intersection of a row and column represents an 'is a' relation between them) and a and i are not the same and the flag which marks the element as already examined is not set, then that flag is set, and procedure finditem is called with i as its parameter. Remember that i is the value of the row. But when finditem is called it is passed to the local variable a in another 'copy' of the procedure. Variable a is the column. So by calling another finditem procedure, at a greater depth of search, we have passed the value of the row variable to the column variable, and thus the next column to be searched will be the one representing the row for which a legal intersection was found. If a is now equal to the target value, low, then flag is set to 1 and control returns to the calling copy of finditem. As that copy also tests to see if flag=1, it will also return to its calling procedure and so on back up the recursive chain until control is passed back to procedure query.

The searching can continue until the nesting limit of the micro is reached (which is surprisingly deep for small programs) or until all the rows in the first examined column have been tested (i.e., variable i in the 'copy' of finditem at the shallowest level of search becomes 50). Line 1360 applies this test. If i does become 50 then the search has failed, flag is not set to 1 and the response 'Not according to my information' is given. (The program hedges its bets somewhat, being unwilling to give a direct 'no' when it may have insufficient information.)

Now what about that odd REM statement in line 780? This actually controls the logical mode by which the program operates. As it stands, with the REM built in, 'is a' relations are only one way. So if we type 'The fisherman is a trainspotter' this does not imply that 'A trainspotter is a fisherman' is also true. The statement 'a king is a monarch' is true, but the statement 'A monarch is a king' is not necessarily true because some monarchs may be queens or princes.

However, you may like the program to operate in such a way that both sides of the equation are regarded as true. For example, the statement 'The twenty-fifth of December is the day before Boxing Day' is true and so is 'The day before Boxing Day is the twenty-fifth of December.' With the REM statement in the program you have to type both these statements to represent their identity, but if the word REMark is removed (not the whole statement, just the keyword 'REMark'), then each input statement is regarded as a statement of identity. Both logical modes have their problems. It is a function of the ambiguity of the word 'is' in English which actually has several quite different meanings, including 'is identical to', 'is similar to', 'is an example of' and 'includes'.

If you wanted to eradicate such difficulties you would need a more complex coding system which dealt with relationships such as 'All kings are monarchs' and 'Some monarchs are kings'. Here we are beginning to enter the world of philosophical logic which, though outside the scope of this book, is by many programmers regarded as one way of coding 'natural' information for the purposes of interpreting questions in natural language. It is easy to see, for example, that simply allowing statements like 'A cook is not a monarch' increases the versatility of the program but it also complicates it enormously. How, for example, would such a program deal with input like 'A king is a monarch', 'The cook is not a monarch', 'The king is a cook', all of which can be simultaneously true. It has to know not only the meaning of 'not' but also the effect of 'the' and 'a'. The second statement actually means something like 'There is a cook who is not a monarch' and the third something like 'There is a king who is a cook.' The program would have to be able to 'think' along the following lines: 'If a king is a monarch and there is at least one king who is a cook and there is at least one cook who is not a monarch then there must be at least two cooks.' Exploring all the implications of this type of programming would take a book of its own.

9 Reasoning, inference and experts

9.1 Inference

So a program which employs such an approach as feature-based semantics needs also to have some rules of 'reasoning'. It will not be able to learn efficiently unless it has rules for manipulating and storing information in an appropriate way. Similarly it will not be able to reason properly if its learning processes are inefficient. It must be able to take in information and store it in a manner most suitable for the kinds of logic it is to apply.

There are two ways to approach the task of coming to conclusions about evidence. One is to gather all the evidence together and consider it as a totality. The Miniex program, given later in this chapter, proceeds in this way. The user must give all the relevant information and then the program attempts to take all that evidence at the same time in order to make its decision. This is what is usually called a parallel approach to the problem. Its main defect is that it requires the user to type in all the necessary information before it can come to any conclusions.

The alternative is a serial approach. In this case only one piece of information is requested at a time and the program attempts to come to a conclusion based only on that information. This has the advantage that the user should only need to provide sufficient information for any given decision and has no need to give superfluous information. The simplest guess would require only one piece of information to be given. For example if the possible outcomes were 'Go for a picnic' and 'Play Scrabble', then the program could ask 'Is it sunny outside?' If the answer were 'yes' it would recommend a picnic; if the answer were 'No' it would suggest a game of Scrabble.

So any piece of information is essentially binary—it represents one of two states. In the parallel approach of Miniex a number of 'yes/no' comparisons are made simultaneously. In the serial approach they are made one at a time, rather as a barrister attempts to extract the truth by gradually whittling away the possibilities, until only one possible answer remains. Suppose, for example, that it was sunny outside but there was also six feet of snow on the ground. In this case the choice of a picnic would probably be inappropriate. The program can conclude that Scrabble is best if it is not sunny, but not that a picnic is best if it is sunny. It needs a further piece of information, a further binary decision.

Suppose we want a simple program which will interrogate a user and draw conclusions about the micro the user is thinking of. The learning involved can be a process of asking questions with 'yes/no' answers and storing the resultant pattern of responses. In such a case at any given point in the interrogation there are only two routes the program can take, so the pattern of reasoning can be represented in binary form. The logic can be held in a form known as a 'binary tree'.

A binary tree is quite simply a hierarchical arrangement of information. For example, if we take the data used in the comparison program and reverse the process, how would we conclude which of the 22 words was being thought of by the user. Suppose we thought it was 'snow'. We could ask as the first question 'Is it hot?' If the answer is 'yes', the 22 possibilities are reduced to 2: tea and fire. If we then ask 'Is it weak?' then if the answer is 'yes' we know the word is 'tea' and if the answer is 'no' we know it is 'fire'. Our reasoning process was something like the tree in Fig. 9.1. So we have worked through our knowledge in the following way:

1. Ask a question.
2. If the answer reduces the alternatives to one then choose that word as the answer.

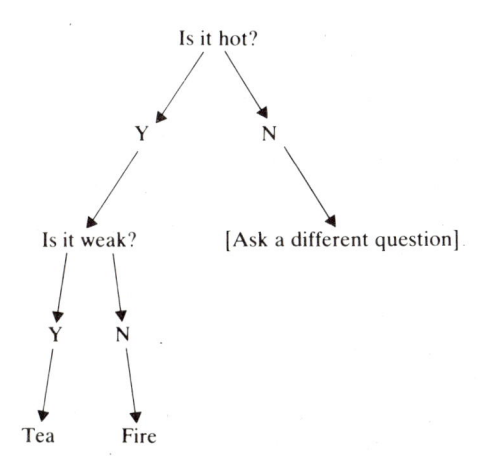

Figure 9.1

3. Otherwise choose the question which will reduce the available alternatives by the greatest amount.

In order to get a program to learn such a strategy (rather than building all the data and logic into the design) we have therefore to tell it not only the answers to the questions it asks but also the questions it should ask. Supposing, for example, that it knows that only a QL has microdrives—but that is all that it knows. It can ask the question 'Does the micro you are thinking of have microdrives?' and if the answer is 'yes' then it can conclude that the micro in question is the QL. But what does it do if it has to go down the other branch of the tree, if the user answers 'no'? It needs another question to ask, such as 'Does the computer have sideways ROMs?' It also needs to know what machine that question would identify and whether 'yes' or 'no' would be the correct answer for such a machine. For the BBC the answer would be 'yes', so once the user has given the program this information it can be stored and the next time round when it receives a 'no' answer to the first question it can ask the new question. But what happens now if the answer to this question is 'no'? There is no question to ask, so a new one is needed.

In this way the program can build up a set of questions and answers to fill in the gaps in its knowledge and it will know that, at any stage in the process of deduction, only three possibilities exist—the user's reply leads to another question, the reply leads to an answer or the reply leads to an empty slot where neither answer nor question exist, in which case the user must fill the gap for the next time round.

So we need a method of representation which has three states and which can point to the appropriate answer or question. We can use a two-dimensional array to represent responses to 'yes' and responses to 'no'. In each element of the array will be a 0 if nothing is known, or a value representing a pointer to either the appropriate question or answer. If we use values under 128 for the questions and over 128 for the answers, then we will know which array any pointer is addressing. If the pointer from any question is less than 128, we can just add the value of the pointer to the value of the question currently being considered to point to an element in the question array where the next question is held. If it is over 127 we do the same for the answer array, as long as we remember to subtract 128 from the value when reading the array.

9.2 Infer—the program

The program Infer (Fig. 9.2) uses this principle of binary information to make its decisions. However, it is also a learning program. It is designed to

```
100 init
110 CLS
120 REPeat aloop
130 found=0
140 failed=0
150 askquest
160 PRINT "Do you want me to guess another micro?"
170 ask
180 IF yn>2 THEN EXIT aloop
190 CLS
200 END REPeat aloop
210 STOP
220 :
230 :
240 DEFine PROCedure init
250 DIM question$(20,40),yes(20),no(20),micro$(20,10)
260 question$(1)="Does it have microdrives?"
270 micro$(1)="QL"
280 entry=1
290 yes(1)=-1
300 no(1)=0
310 free=1
320 query=1
330 END DEFine init
340 :
350 :
360 DEFine PROCedure askquest
370 count=1
380 REPeat bloop
390 checkans
400 IF answer$(1)="Y" OR answer$(1)="y" THEN yescode
410 IF answer$(1)="N" OR answer$(1)="n" THEN nocode
420 IF found=1 OR failed=1 THEN EXIT bloop
```

Figure 9.2 (*continues*)

```
430 END REPeat bloop
440 END DEFine askquest
450 :
460 :
470 DEFine PROCedure yescode
480 IF yes(count)=0 THEN failure:RETurn
490 IF yes(count)<0 THEN succeed(-yes(count)):RETurn
500 count=yes(count)
510 END DEFine yescode
520 :
530 :
540 DEFine PROCedure nocode
550 IF no(count)=0 THEN failure:RETurn
560 IF no(count)<0 THEN succeed(-no(count)):RETurn
570 count=no(count)
580 END DEFine nocode
590 :
600 :
610 DEFine PROCedure failure
620 failmess
630 IF yn<3 THEN
640 yes(count)=entry+1
650 ELSE
660 no(count)=entry+1
670 END IF
680 fail2
690 IF yn<3 THEN
700 yes(entry)=-free
710 REMark no(entry)=0
720 ELSE
730 REMark yes(entry)=0
740 no(entry)=-free
750 END IF
760 END DEFine failure
770 :
780 :
```

Figure 9.2 (*continues*)

```
790 DEFine PROCedure fail2
800 PRINT "For a ";newmicro$;" what is the answer to :"
810 PRINT ident$
820 ask
830 entry=entry+1
840 failed=1
850 END DEFine fail2
860 :
870 :
880 DEFine PROCedure failmess
890 PRINT "I have never heard of such a micro"
900 INPUT "What is it?",newmicro$
910 INPUT"What question would identify a ";(newmicro$);" ?",ident$
920 free=free+1
930 micro$(free)=newmicro$
940 query=query+1
950 question$(query)=ident$
960 END DEFine failmess
970 :
980 :
990 DEFine PROCedure checkans
1000 PRINT question$(count)
1010 ask
1020 answer$=text$
1030 END DEFine checkans
1040 :
1050 :
1060 DEFine PROCedure ask
1070 REPeat cloop
1080 INPUT text$
1090 IF text$="" THEN GO TO 1080
1100 yn= text$(1) INSTR "YyNn"
1110 IF yn <>0 THEN EXIT cloop
1120 END REPeat cloop
1130 END DEFine ask
```

Figure 9.2 (*continues*)

```
1140 :
1150 :
1160 DEFine PROCedure succeed(mic)
1170 PRINT "Is it a ";micro$(mic)
1180 ask
1190 IF yn>2 THEN fail3(mic):RETurn
1200 PRINT "It was obvious, really"
1210 found=1
1220 END DEFine succeed
1230 :
1240 :
1250 DEFine PROCedure fail3(mic)
1260 failmess
1270 IF answer$(1)="Y" OR answer$(1)="y" THEN
1280 yes(count)=query
1290 ELSE
1300 no(count)=query
1310 END IF
1320 fail2
1330 reply$=text$
1340 IF reply$(1)="Y" OR reply$(1)="y" THEN
1350 yes(entry)=-free
1360 no(entry)=-mic
1370 ELSE
1380 yes(entry)=-mic
1390 no(entry)=-free
1400 END IF
1410 END DEFine fail3
```

Figure 9.2

guess the name of the microcomputer you are thinking of but initially only knows about one micro, the QL. It asks the question 'Does it have microdrives?' If you answer 'yes' it thinks it knows the answer so says 'Is it a QL?' If you then say 'yes' it gives you a self-satisfied message. If, however, you answer 'no' at either of these two stages it has a problem. It knows about no other machines and it knows no other questions to ask.

So it admits its ignorance and asks the user to tell it the name of the micro in question. It then asks for a question it could use to identify that micro and for the correct answer to that question. Suppose we answered 'no' to the question 'Does it have microdrives?' because we were thinking of a BBC micro (wash your mouth out with soap and water). We tell it 'BBC' and give as a suitable distinguishing question 'Is it made by Acorn?' The answer to this question is 'yes' so next time round if we answer 'no' to the first question it will ask us about Acorn. If we reply that it was made by Acorn it will suggest that the machine in question is a BBC. If, by some chance, we were thinking of the Atom or the Electron or one of the ABC machines we would say 'no', so it would again repeat the business of asking for information about this micro, which is new to its database.

The program is thus constructing a binary tree. At each node of the tree there are only two possible responses from the user—yes or no. In each case the user's response either suggests a particular micro or leads to the next question to ask. These are the next nodes in the tree. At each node there are two possible outcomes and these branch continually until they either hit a correct answer or they find a 'No data' slot. In the first case the congratulatory message is printed. In the second the new data is requested and the database updated.

How does this work in reality? Firstly init creates the arrays and declares the initial pointers. Array question$ holds the questions to ask, yes holds the pointers for positive answers, no holds the pointers for negative answers, micro$ holds the names of the micros that the program has learned. The first element of question$ holds the first question, the first element of micro$ holds the name of the first micro and the pointers in yes(1) and no(1) hold pointers for the answer to question 1. (These pointers are explained below.)

The main loop of lines 120 to 200 cycles continually asking questions and guessing micros until the user decides he or she has had enough. Each cycle first calls procedure askquest, which in turn calls procedure checkans. This prints the current question, pointed to by the variable count. The first time askquest is called count is 1 so the first question is asked. Procedure ask is called simply to ensure that the answer is 'yes' or 'no' by only allowing input of the letters 'y' and 'n'.

The reply to this question is stored in answer$ and control backs up to askquest. Lines 400 and 410 then test for the possible actions resulting from 'yes' or 'no' answers. In the first case 'yescode' is called, in the second 'nocode'. Both carry out essentially the same operation, namely testing their branch of the binary tree. Element count of the relevant array, yes or no, is tested. Remember that count is initially 1. If the element holds a positive number, i.e., a number greater than 0, then count is simply increased to that number, control backs up to askquest, and the next question is asked.

However, the first time around element yes(1) holds −1 and element no(1) holds 0 (declared in lines 290 and 300). These are codes which represent the action to be taken as a response to this answer.

There are actually three possible actions:

1. print the next question;
2. print 'Is it a ???';
3. request new data.

As we have seen, a positive number can be used as a pointer to the next question (possibility (1)). If we use 0 to represent no information available, then this results in possibility (3). A negative number can represent a pointer to the array micro$ (i.e., the second possibility). So for the first question 'no' gives code 0, so the program needs to ask for additional data. This is done by calling procedure failure.

'Yes', on the other hand, gives code −1. This calls procedure succeed with the negative of yes(count) as its parameter. In this case yes(count) is −1, so its negative is 1. Procedure succeed now prints the question 'Is it a QL?' It is using the parameter stored in yes(count) to point to the micro in micro$, i.e., micro$(1). Procedure ask is here called again to get the 'yes' or 'no' answer. If the answer is 'no' then procedure fail is called. If 'yes', the smug message is displayed, a flag called 'found' is set to 1 and control backs up to the main loop.

There are consequently two kinds of failure and therefore two types of action which can be taken. The first failure comes if a question is answered and no further question or micro is pointed to by the array for that answer. Procedure failure firstly calls procedure failmess which prints the 'failed' message, then asks for the name of the micro and a question that will identify it. A variable called free, which points to the next free space in the array micro$, is incremented by 1 and the name of the new micro is placed in that element. A second variable, query, holds a pointer to the next free space in array question$. The identifying question is stored in this element (lines 920 to 950).

Control returns to procedure failure. If the answer to the last 'yes/no' question (i.e., the one at which the program failed) was 'yes', then yes(count) is changed to point to the new question. If the answer was 'no', then it is no(count) which is changed. Procedure fail2 now asks for the answer to the new question which discriminates the new micro. Variable entry is increased by 1 and a flag called failed is set.

Control returns to failure, which now sets either no(entry) or yes(entry) to

−free according to whether the discriminating answer was 'yes' or 'no'. Remember free points to a micro and that this is held as a negative value in the arrays yes and no. The opposite array element is reset to 0 to signify 'no data available if this answer is given'. Control then backs up to the main loop again.

In the case of failure at the point where a specific micro is proved incorrect, the program must not only add pointers to a new question and answer but must also change the existing pointer so that the new question is asked instead of the 'Is it x micro?' question. The first part of fail3 is therefore the same as for failure. As fail3 receives as a parameter the element number of the micro which has just been asked about and the variable free holds the element number of the new micro, the current pointer for the previous answer must become a pointer to the new question (instead of the micro it currently points to), and the next answers in yes and no will be pointers to one of the two micros.

Let us work through an example to explain this. Suppose the program asks 'Is it a BBC?' If the answer is 'no' then it has failed. As 'BBC micro' is held in micro$(2), the value 2 is passed to fail3. The program says it does not know of the micro and asks for the new name. We say 'Electron' and the distinguishing question is 'Does it have Mode 7?' 'Electron' is stored in micro$(3) (because variable free points to element (3)) and 'Does it have Mode 7?' is stored in question$(3) because query is 3.

The user's last response was 'no', so at line 1300 the current pointer for the no array is changed from −2 (pointer to 'BBC') to +3 (pointer to new question). Now the user has to give the correct answer to 'Does it have Mode 7?' The answer is 'no'. So the next no element, which is no(entry) is set to the value for the Electron (−3) while yes(entry) is set to the value for BBC (−2). Obviously if the answer to 'Does it have Mode 7?' is correct, then it points to the new machine, but if incorrect it points to the old machine which would previously have been the conclusion before this new question.

When all this has been done control backs up to the main loop again and the whole process is repeated.

9.3 Expert systems

An expert system, sometimes called an Intelligent Knowledge Based System (or IKBS to shorten the mouthful), is essentially a computer system containing expertise in a particular area. Usually it is a diagnostic system of some kind so that, given an appropriate set of information it will make some form of judgement or recommendation or, if it cannot do either of these, it will ask for further information which it thinks will help it make such a judgement.

Typical expert systems range from MYCIN, one of the oldest of expert systems, which is used for diagnosing blood infections and will make recommendations for treatment, to Prospector, a system used in searching for minerals, which gained a certain fame for expert systems when it correctly predicted a multi-million-dollar site of molybdenum on a site which was being used for the dumping of waste, to PECOS and ROSIE which are aids in programming and designing expert systems respectively. There is no reason in principle why any area of human knowledge could not be put into such a system and be used for diagnosing and predicting certain results given certain information. Of course there are huge problems with this. Much of what we call knowledge is not really knowledge at all but a mish-mash of assumptions, beliefs and misunderstandings. Much of what we know we cannot describe. For example, I know how to swim, how to ride a bicycle and how to sing 'Yellow Submarine' (though some might dispute the last point) yet I cannot say what it is I know or how I am able to use that knowledge. Even where people can say something about their knowledge they often cannot say everything and they find it difficult to put what they know into a form that could readily be processed by an expert system.

So there is a rapidly growing band of computer scientists cum interviewers who are known as 'knowledge engineers'. Their task is to use every technique known in order to extract relevant information from the expert and code it into the machine. Because of the difficulty of the task of the knowledge engineer, two basic approaches to building expert systems have come about. The first is to extract all the necessary and relevant information, then code it and finally build a system around it. This is a relatively fixed system whose data is unchanging and which requires a great deal of work (and, funnily enough, expertise) from the knowledge engineer to be built. However, once completed such a system is usually pretty robust and likely to work consistently within the tolerances that businesses and professions require.

The second approach is becoming more popular in the ordinary day-to-day world of complex and varied problems. This is to build a general-purpose expert system which can, theoretically at least, cope with a large range of types of information. It then has to learn all about the area it is to be used in until it can perform satisfactorily in that area. It learns by interrogating the expert who is to use it, using some of the techniques of the knowledge engineer and a process called induction. Induction is simply learning by example. We all learn by induction. That was how I learned to swim, to ride a bike and to sing 'Yellow Submarine'.

It works like this. The computer asks the expert for some possible outcomes that it would be expected to predict, and some possible events that might be related to those outcomes. It then combines the events in different ways and asks the user to estimate the likelihood of the possible outcomes. For example, if we gave it the outcomes 'Switches off TV', 'Turns up volume' and 'Switches to other channel', and the possible events 'Party Political Broadcast', 'Soap Opera', 'Computer Programme' and 'News Bulletin' it might ask 'Given a "Party Political Broadcast" on Channel 1 and a "Soap Opera" on Channel 2, what is the probability that the watcher will switch off?'

Ideally, of course, the computer will present every possible combination of events and ask for estimates of every possible set of outcomes, but this will simply lead to yet another combinatorial explosion and the user will be perpetually feeding information to the machine as it discovers yet another possible combination. Instead it must contain various rules for relating pieces of information and combining probabilities. Naturally it should explore as many cases as seem feasible but, with luck, it will not need information on every possible case before it can become a workable system. As you feed in more and more examples, it learns more and more about the logic and probability of their relationships and it becomes more adept at predicting likely outcomes. However, there is always the chance that some freak combination of events has been overlooked, so a learning system is intrinsically less reliable than a custom-built system. At the same time learning systems are much more flexible. If such a freak combination of events does occur it is usually possible to wipe the blood off the floor and add that set of information to the program and make it that bit more efficient.

The rules which do this learning are generally simple in principle but complex in practice. Either they are statistical (what is the probability of y, given x?) or logical (if A and B and C then D). Or both kinds can be used together. Essentially both kinds of rule are the same—how is one item dependent on another? The question is whether to build the system around numbers or around logic. The complexity comes when several rules interrelate. If it was merely a question of 'Find the condition, then look up the result' expert systems would have been around for a long time. And, in this sense they have been around for a lot longer than computers. A car manual, a first-aid handbook and a social-security leaflet are all examples of systems which are meant to help you if certain conditions occur. You look up the problem in the index and find the page with the answer. So these are primitive expert systems, but they do not do any of the work for you.

9.4 Heuristics

Seldom is it possible to give exact rules for combinations of probabilities, and few expert systems will give you certain predictions when they are run. Systems using statistics based on methods using 'Bayesian probability' will often give a number of different conclusions with degrees of probability against each. It is up to the human operator to act on the most probable prediction or, more likely, incorporate that prediction in his or her own decision making. It has been estimated that an expert on his own will achieve about 80 per cent success in a particular field of prediction, that an expert system on its own can also achieve about the same, but that expert and expert system hand in hand can achieve over 90 per cent success. This is largely because the system is better at remembering all the information and examining all the permutations, but a human being still has thought processes (such as intuition and creativity) which expert systems cannot satisfactorily model.

However, such systems increasingly incorporate sets of rules which attempt to capture some of the more peculiar features of human thinking and decision making. These are the rules we have glanced at several times already in this book, generally called heuristics, that is 'rules of thumb'. They are rules for making guesses or for guiding judgement and there is no single way of describing or classifying them. Often they are simple lists of actions which 'fire' when certain conditions are true. They are placed at every point in the program where it is found necessary to have them, and may govern all aspects of control and data manipulation in the program. They differ from the more rigid statistical and logical rules which traditionally form the heart of expert systems in being much less rigid and *ad hoc*. Instead of representing tried and tested probability formulae they are more like the following:

If the current idea seems to be a better one than the previous idea then try taking it to extremes.

If there is nothing else to do, then choose a random rule from a list of rules which previously gave results in a different area.

Of course the actual programming does not look like this but these are typical translations. Some major successes using heuristics like these have been made by programs called AM and Eurisko, written by Douglas Lenat.

The first was a program designed to 'discover' interesting mathematical formulae. Eurisko is a general-purpose system which, amongst other things, consistently won an American wargames championship by designing superior fleets of space ships. It made clever discoveries such as realizing that the rules of the competition allowed ships to fire on themselves. It then examined the implications of what seems like a rather silly quirk of the rules and eventually discovered that, if the weakest ship in a fleet destroyed itself the fleet would be able to travel more rapidly because a fleet always travels at the speed of its slowest ship. A wounded ship therefore adversely affected the whole fleet, so if it destroyed itself the fleet as a whole benefitted.

Having learned all about these rules and how to design the ships (rules which have been changed successively each year to cope with the flexibility of the program) it was then able to take some of the same 'ideas' (or heuristics) that it had learned in wargaming to the problem of designing a new microchip. In designing space fleets it had learned that a potentially useful heuristic was something like 'To improve overall performance make the system symmetrical'. It applied this rule to the problem of chip design and created a new type of chip, the three-dimensional chip, symmetrical not only in two dimensions but also the third, an idea human designers had never explored. In other words it learned examples from one field of knowledge, and used the rules it had learned to come up with a totally original idea in another field. You will recognize this as another example of bisociation.

One final feature that an expert system should have is some way of justifying itself. Eurisko, for example uses a complex windowing system which allows the user to view all the processes currently going on in the program. The user can also interrupt the program and alter information, or direct the program to change its line of investigation, or to alter its data. Most commercial expert systems give the user opportunity for extracting an account of its reasoning chain—both the original data on which the judgements are made and the rules it has been applying at each stage in order to make its series of connected judgements. This feature is important for novice or inexpert users as they often need to know how a decision was arrived at to know how accurate it might be, and to understand the nature of the decision. As the whole point of widespread expert systems is to make expertise available to non-experts it is important that the user can feel confident in the decisions arrived at and in his or her undertanding of the processes involved. It is also important that the user should be able to override the system's judgements on temporary occasions (rather than permanently altering the system or its data) so, just as with other aspects of

AI, integrating such features as natural language understanding and other aspects of user-friendliness becomes more and more important in expert systems.

Let us now look at a mini-system of our own. There is no room to produce a fully-fledged system but you should be able to see some of the principles illustrated in the program given as Fig. 9.3 and also how it can be improved by taking account of some of the other elements of AI we have already discussed.

```
100 CLS
110 setup
120 learn
130 REPeat qloop
140 PRINT \\"Do you want me to make a guess?"
150 yn$=INKEY$
160 IF yn$="" THEN GO TO 150
170 IF yn$ INSTR "YyNn">2 THEN EXIT qloop
180 CLS
190 prediction
200 END REPeat qloop
210 STOP
220 :
230 DEFine PROCedure setup
240 CLS
250 REPeat sloop
260 PRINT\\ "How many outcomes or"!" results are possible?"
270 INPUT outcome
280 IF outcome<9 AND outcome>1 THEN EXIT sloop
290 IF outcome>8 THEN
300 PRINT "Too many"
310 ELSE
320 PRINT "Not enough"
330 END IF
340 END REPeat sloop
350 CLS
```

Figure 9.3 (*continues*)

```
360 REPeat vloop
370 PRINT\\ "How many variables or conditions"!" can affect these outcomes?"
380 INPUT condition
390 IF condition<9 AND condition>1 THEN EXIT vloop
400 IF condition >8 THEN
410 PRINT "Too many"
420 ELSE
430 PRINT "Not enough"
440 END IF
450 END REPeat vloop
460 CLS
470 DIM result(outcome,condition),resultname$(outcome,40)
480 DIM condname$(condition,40),temp(condition)
490 FOR i=1 TO outcome
500 CLS
510 AT 3,0:PRINT "What is the name of result number ";:STRIP 7:INK 0:PRINT i;:STRIP 2:INK 7:PRINT "?"
520 INPUT resultname$(i)
530 NEXT i
540 FOR i =1 TO condition
550 CLS
560 AT 3,0:PRINT "What is the name of"!" condition number ";:STRIP 7:INK 0:PRINT i;:STRIP 2:INK 7:PRINT "?"
570 INPUT condname$(i)
580 NEXT i
590 gstrg$="@123456789"&CHR$(10)
600 num$="@"
610 END DEFine setup
620 :
630 DEFine PROCedure learn
640 CLS
```

Figure 9.3 (*continues*)

```
650 PRINT\\ "Now you have to educate me"
660 FOR i=1 TO condition
670 FOR j=1 TO outcome
680 PRINT\ "Could ";condname$(i);" result in ";resultname$(j);"?"
690 REPeat gloop
700 yn$=INKEY$
710 IF yn$="" THEN GO TO 700
720 yn=yn$ INSTR "@YyNn"
730 IF yn>1 THEN EXIT gloop
740 END REPeat gloop
750 IF yn<3 THEN result(j,i)=1
760 NEXT j
770 NEXT i
780 END DEFine learn
790 :
800 DEFine PROCedure prediction
810 PRINT "Which of these conditions apply?"
820 nstring$=""
830 FOR i = 1 TO condition
840 temp(i)=0
850 PRINT\ i;" ";condname$(i)
860 NEXT i
870 PRINT\ "Type the number of the condition"
880 PRINT "         or <Return> to end"
890 num$="@"
900 REPeat outloop
910 REPeat inloop
920 n$=INKEY$
930 IF n$="" THEN GO TO 920
940 IF (n$ INSTR gstrg$ >1 AND n$ INSTR num$<1) OR n$=CHR$(10) THEN EXIT inloop
950 END REPeat inloop
960 IF n$=CHR$(10) THEN EXIT outloop
970 num$=num$ & n$
980 x=n$
```

Figure 9.3 (*continues*)

```
 990 temp(x)=1
1000 END REPeat outloop
1010 match
1020 END DEFine prediction
1030 :
1040 DEFine PROCedure match
1050 score=0
1060 poor=0
1070 best=0
1080 worst=0
1090 v=1
1100 REPeat vloop
1110 h=1
1120 tempscore=0
1130 temppoor=0
1140 REPeat hloop
1150 IF result(v,h)=temp(h) THEN
1160 tempscore=tempscore+1
1170 ELSE
1180 temppoor=temppoor+1
1190 END IF
1200 IF h=condition THEN EXIT hloop
1210 h=h+1
1220 END REPeat hloop
1230 IF temppoor>=poor THEN
1240 poor=temppoor
1250 worst=v
1260 END IF
1270 IF tempscore>=score THEN
1280 score=tempscore
1290 best=v
1300 END IF
1310 IF v=outcome THEN EXIT vloop
1320 v=v+1
1330 END REPeat vloop
1340 IF score=condition THEN
1350 exact
1360 ELSE
```

Figure 9.3 (*continues*)

```
1370  bestmatch
1380  END IF
1390  END DEFine match
1400  :
1410  DEFine PROCedure exact
1420  CLS
1430  PRINT "These conditions result in ";resultname$(best)
1440  END DEFine exact
1450  :
1460  DEFine PROCedure bestmatch
1470  CLS
1480  PRINT "I don´t know the answer but:"
1490  PRINT\"the opposite of ";resultname$(worst);" might be "!"the case (if that makes sense) ";
1500  negcent=(poor/condition)*100
1510  PRINT "with a likelihood of ";negcent;"%"
1520  percent=(score/condition)*100
1530  IF score>0 THEN PRINT " and ";resultname$(best);" is a possibility with a likelihood of ";percent;"%"
1540  END DEFine bestmatch
```

Figure 9.3

9.5 Miniex

This program is an example of an expert shell because it can be used for many applications. Its usefulness depends entirely on the nature and value of the information given to it by the user and it works in a sledgehammer manner by asking the user who sets it up to give all the information it needs.

   Procedure setup as usual dimensions arrays and fills them with values. However, this is done in an interactive way. The user is asked to provide the parameters for the program and these are used to establish the nature of the program's storage. Firstly the user must supply the number of possible results or outcomes that are being considered. For example, if we wanted an expert system to diagnose illness, the number of outcomes would be the number of possible illnesses that could be diagnosed. If we wanted a system to classify botanical specimens, then the number of outcomes would be the number of possible classifications which could be made.

The program allows a range of only two to eight outcomes. Obviously if there is only one outcome there is no prediction involved because the outcome is certain. More than eight outcomes is certainly possible, but means an awful lot of work for the user in later stages of the program.

In a similar way the number of variables or conditions is asked for. These would be the various symptoms in the case of our illness system or the various features a botanical sample could have in the case of our plant classifying system. Again the system arbitrarily limits the number to eight.

The following arrays are then dimensioned. The array 'result' has one cell for every condition and every result (i.e., the number of conditions times the number of possible results). The array resultname$ is to hold the names of all the possible outcomes, condname$ to hold the names of all the possible conditions. Temp is to hold temporary values for each condition. Lines 490 to 580 then ask the user to name all the outcomes and conditions and this information is placed in the arrays.

The program is now ready to 'learn' about the situation the user has set up. It proceeds in a very simple way. For each possible condition and each possible outcome it asks if that condition could result in that outcome. So, for example, if the condition was 'patient has headache' and the possible outcome was 'influenza' the user must type 'y' because a headache can be a symptom of 'flu. A headache does not necessarily mean that the patient has 'flu, nor does having 'flu necessarily mean that the user has a headache, but there is a possible connection between them. Each positive answer is stored in the result array at the cell representing the intersection of that condition and that result.

In this way the result array will gradually be filled with a pattern of 1s and 0s, representing 'yes' (condition x is associated with result z) or 'no', (there is no such link). When the array is full the program is ready to predict (or guess!) the outcome of a particular set of conditions.

Procedure prediction does this guessing. Firstly it prints out all the condition names with a number by each and clears the temporary array which will hold a 1 or 0 for each condition. The user must type the numbers of all conditions that apply in this particular case. In order to make the program a little friendly a revamped input routine is used to ensure that the same number is not typed twice. The input numbers are held as a string called num$. However, this string is used only for checking the remaining input. The key part of the input routine is line 990, in which the temporary slot for that condition is set to 1.

Procedure 'match' is then called to compare the input with the patterns held in result. This is also quite a simple procedure. Its aim is ideally to find an exact match between the pattern of 1s held in temp and a pattern held in result. If it finds such a match, then it will predict that the outcome for which that pattern of results holds is the outcome. But the ideal cannot always be achieved. So there is also a bestmatch procedure which tries to find plausible outcomes which are not, according to the data the program has, certain.

Two loops are used to do this. The core of the comparison is lines 1150 to 1190, where each column in the result table is cycled through in turn. If a match is found between that and the current element of temp, then the variable tempscore is increased by 1 (i.e., if element temp(h) is 0 and element result (v,h) = 0, then a match is found or if element temp(h) = 1 and element result(v,h) = 1 a match is also found). If there is no match another variable, temppoor is incremented. The outside loop, vloop cycles through each row in the array. If, for the current row, the value for tempscore is higher than for another variable, score, then score becomes the new value. In this way the program remembers the highest number of matches found, because this is the value of score when all columns and all rows have been compared. It is also necessary to remember which row had that highest score because this is the best match, so this information is held in the variable 'best'. Similarly a second pair of variables, poor and worst, hold the row for which the least number of matches are found.

When all rows and columns have been examined, then the test in line 1340 will call procedure exact if score (the highest number of matches) is equal to condition (the total number of possible conditions). This is true only when every element in a given column matches. If the test fails the procedure bestmatch is called.

The procedure exact simply prints out the name of the result for which the exact match was found. Note, however, that if two exact matches are found only the first one is remembered. This is a defect of the system. The procedure bestmatch uses a couple of simple heuristics to suggest possible outcomes. Firstly it says that it has no exact match and then it suggests that the opposite of the worst case might be the result. In some instances this could be true. For example, if we want to know which of two teams will win a match and our conditions do not equate with either team winning the match, then one possibility is that the team with the fewest correspondences between possible and actual conditions will lose. It might not be possible to say conclusively that England will win the test but one possibility is that Australia will not win (because Australia has fewest correspondences). A crude percentage is given

REASONING, INFERENCE AND EXPERTS 169

to give some idea of how plausible the suggestion might be, but this should not be regarded as a serious statistical probability.

The other likely possibility is of course the result with the best match even if it was not exact. However, neither of these two procedures is much use in poor cases. They only help if the match is very close or very far away. If, for example, all the outcomes match on four conditions out of eight then the program might conclude that one possibility is 'x' because it matched 50% of the conditions and another possibility is 'the opposite of x' because it failed to match 50 per cent of the time. Not very helpful.

Hopefully you will get a flavour of the nature of expert systems from Miniex without having to understand any complex logic or statistics. However, you should also be able to see that probabilities are not straightforward. They are neither easy to predict nor always easy to interpret. The more uncertain the available information, the less useful the resulting judgement by the program, and this is true not only of Miniex but also more elaborate expert systems. It seems therefore that the expert systems of the future will operate a combination of methods, using probability theory, logic and heuristics which are proven in particular cases.

10 Personal computers with personalities

10.1 Personality and intelligence

One of the peculiarities of human beings is the odd combination of characteristics we call personality. Making a machine like a human being means at the very least that it must understand personality and be able to respond appropriately to different types of personality. A more complete version of the human machine would be one that had a personality itself—but this is not necessarily a desirable feature as for most practical purposes personalities tend to get in the way of objectivity and efficiency. However, the search for a truly user-friendly system may lead researchers to decide that certain types of 'personality' are appropriate to certain kinds of task where communicating with real human beings takes place. For example, medical consultant programs may feel more satisfactory to the patient if they are 'understanding' and 'supportive'. Coaching programs may benefit from an appropriate blend of aggression and persuasion. Financial advice may be more effective if conveyed in a suitably serious manner. Just as everyone has different styles of communication for different situations, so, if we are to have user-friendly micros in different situations, we may want them to have suitable personalities to communicate in suitable styles.

Some people would say that personality has nothing to do with intelligence, or at least that intelligence is just one aspect of personality and so AI should not be concerned with wider aspects of human personality. This would be a mistaken view for several reasons. In the first place, as I have said, the primary goal of AI is to understand human psychology by providing computer models, not necessarily to create human machines. A machine with a convincing personality would only be a side effect of the real psychological research.

Secondly it does not seem to be true that intelligence is a simple quality that people either have or do not have as part of their overall personality. I hope this book shows that intelligence is a whole variety of different but interrelated characteristics and certainly cannot be simply expressed. It has been shown, for example, that IQ tests do very little in the way of measuring intelligence. All they can claim to do is to measure IQ, i.e., they measure someone's skill in solving IQ tests! IQ is one aspect of intelligence, an important one for certain kinds of problems and activities but totally irrelevant, even obstructive in other situations. If you read any biography of a so-called Great Man or Woman, you will find that IQ has relatively little to do with their success even in cases where one might expect it to be very important, such as for generals and politicians. For everyday practical problems qualities which are much more difficult to define come into play, qualities which are usually grouped together under the general heading of 'personality'.

Thirdly there are areas of AI which require some personality theory in order to be adequate in themselves. For example, neither natural language understanding nor natural language production could hope to be comprehensive without some in-built representation of personality, particularly the personal connotations that certain words and phrases have. Even the major AI success of speech production suffers largely because speech chips and speech algorithms lack intonation. Intonation is expressive of mood, attitude and intention and these are all features of personality.

Finally, even if intelligence and personality were separate things, there are many reasons why we might want computers to have personalities in order to modify their intelligence. You could say that a user-friendly program was one which was more intelligent than a human being in a particular area and which had a 'front end' or 'user interface' which personalized that intelligence in such a way that each particular user could obtain responses easily and without feeling 'inferior' or frustrated. The two major drawbacks of human experts from the point of view of human non-experts are their apparent superiority and their peculiar language. Both these should be avoided in computer experts if attention is paid to the way the computer expresses its information and to the way the user asks for such information.

There are other less practical but no less exciting reasons for trying to get machines to understand and possess personalities. I have already mentioned the academic desire to understand human personality, with its very important results for clinical psychology, psychotherapy and psychiatry. More frivolous is the desire to give ordinary people machines which can be companions (though the extent to which people may want mechanical companions is unknown) and to create games which employ personality features.

Both of these latter aims may seem trivial, but they may not be. A society should be criticized if there are people within it who are so lonely that they need mechanical companions, but the fact is that Western society is constructed this way and likely to become more so. There are many lonely and frustrated people who find companionship only in pets or withdraw into mental disorder of some kind and it seems unlikely that any industrial society, whether totalitarian, communist or democratic, can provide such people with sufficient aid. There are also occasions when most people would welcome interaction with a 'personality' of their choosing rather than the ones they find around them, either through boredom or the desire for some new form of stimulus. Any machine which could even partially satisfy such a need could be a great boon and could have great therapeutic value. (It should be added, however, that such machines could also be used as instruments of control and that they might cause as much psychological harm as good if designed badly or used in inappropriate ways.)

But this is entering the world of science fiction, for no such machines exist or are likely to exist within a few years. Before we scoff, however, we should remember the pace of technological change. Hardware developments are rapid, even increasing exponentially in some areas. Whilst it is unlikely that this will remain so for a very long time, it will continue for five or ten years so that the machines which we can barely envisage now will almost certainly be available within that period. Software is, however, not developing at anything like the same rate. Even the very recent 'software explosion' has consisted largely of production of many different versions of the same idea rather than continual leap-frogging developments of new ideas. No one can predict where software will go or what software will be developed in ten years, but it seems likely that, if hardware does continue to develop and to drop in price at the same rate, intelligent and personalized software will be available in about that period. One of the interesting features of trends like this is that guesses and predictions often have the effect of coming true because the developers think 'that's a good idea' and start to work on it. They never realize how difficult the task is or how long it will take when they start and they never produce what they intended to produce, but one can almost guarantee that if enough people talk about 'software with personality' or 'software that understands personality' in 1985 then there will be something like it by 1995.

10.2 Building a personality program

We will not attempt anything so sophisticated as giving the micro its own personality. Instead let us first explore what might be involved in giving the characters in a game some rudiments of personality. Such a feature would be most useful in text-based games, particularly adventures and simulations, though wargames would also benefit from incorporating the personalities of leaders into some of the decision-making processes and even arcade games could possess sprites with personality, though their feelings are more likely to be expressed graphically than verbally and therefore demand a high degree of graphic resolution or a very simple personality model.

To explain this last idea a little further—suppose you had a conventional Pacman game in which there were more ghosts than usual, each a different colour. Instead of collecting a power pill to enable Pacman to devour all the ghosts, each ghost could have four personality states:

1. angry—devours Pacman;
2. hostile—obstructs Pacman;
3. friendly—will let Pacman past;
4. helpful—will eat dots for Pacman.

Each of the states can be shown by some graphical equivalent of the state such as a grin, a smile, a scowl and a violent rage, or by changing colour, flashing, etc. A ghost will be turned from one state to another by Pacman's actions. For example, suppose all the ghosts start off in the hostile state. Each time Pacman bumps into a ghost the ghost will become more annoyed (i.e., the variable 'state-of-ghost' will be decremented) and when that variable reaches a certain value the ghost becomes angry and will devour Pacman if touched by him.

On the other hand if Pacman gives a ghost a treasure (treasures will be scattered around the maze) then state-of-ghost will be incremented. When it reaches a threshold value the ghost becomes friendly and lets Pacman past. Given more treasures it will eventually become helpful and start to eat the dots for Pacman. Complexity can be added to such a game by interrelating the 'personalities' of the ghosts such that, if one becomes hostile another becomes friendly, and if one becomes helpful two become hostile. Similarly Pacman must make a decision whether to keep the treasures (and thus increase his score) or to give them to a ghost and thus increase its helpfulness.

This rather elementary game illustrates some of the fundamentals of personality, albeit in a very simple way. It shows that personality is really a set of 'states of mind' and that those states change according to situation *and* according to the predisposition (or preprogramming) of a character. Giving a character in a game a personality is therefore equivalent to describing all the states it can be in and the conditions under which it will change from one state to another. This seems to make sense from the human point of view as well. We say someone is 'violent', for example, either if they are currently smashing the furniture or if they are likely to smash the furniture, i.e., they are currently 'in a state' or they are predisposed to pass into that state. We also recognize that passage into certain states is conditional on certain events ('If you take all his Heavy Metal records he will smash the furniture because he is a violent type').

The game also shows that personality is of no interest to anyone unless that personality interacts with the world around it and particularly with other people or characters. In fact most of the characteristics we regard as features of personality involve some form of relationship or interaction. 'Loving' or 'hating', 'aggressive' or 'submissive', 'greedy' or 'unselfish' are not simply states of mind. They are ways of interacting with the world and with people.

So, from a design point of view, the value of a model of personality rests solely in the types of interaction it creates. There is no point in building in a detailed model of jealousy, revenge and hatred in a program designed to sort shopping lists into alphabetical order. There is no point in building a model of political motivation into a program with no political component. Personality interaction in a program can be of two kinds, as illustrated again by our sample game. It can be interaction between programmed characters and the player (or the character controlled by the player), e.g., between Pacman and the ghosts, or it can be interaction simply between characters without intervention from the player, e.g., between the ghosts themselves.

There are many personality variables. If you were simply to jot down the main characteristics of people you know you would rapidly create a long list of variables and this list will probably suggest more, such as the opposites of all these qualities. A quick glance at a thesaurus will show that there are literally hundreds of words expressing personal qualities of one kind or another. Consequently there are many approaches to programming personality.

One of the earliest, and in some ways one of the most successful, attempts to put a person into a computer was Kenneth Colby's **PARRY** program. Colby was interested in the nature of paranoia, so in order to find out more about it he built the program **PARRY** which simulates the responses of a paranoid patient to questioning by the user. **PARRY** was quite a convincing model of the illness, so much so that it partially passed the Turing test. Output from the program was given to a number of psychiatrists together with output from conversations with real paranoiacs. They were asked to decide which were transcripts of real paranoid output. Discrimination between the real and the fake paranoid was not better than chance so, on the evidence of that single text, **PARRY** was judged to be an equivalent human being. However, in many ways the test is not fair (and certainly not as convincing as the full Turing test would be) because the psychiatrists had no opportunity to interrogate the patient themselves, nor to frame the conversation which led to the text. Diagnosis, especially in psychiatry, can depend very much on the particular questions asked and the situation in which they are asked.

What PARRY does is to 'mistrust' its interrogators and to interpret remarks suspiciously or hostilely, as Colby had observed paranoiacs do. It looks for keywords in input which, according to the paranoid delusion, index some harm or threat, and it may move from some innocent topic which is connected to one of these threatening topics because it is always expecting the delusion to be confirmed by what people say. Its output may be neutral, but becomes more hostile, hypersensitive, uncooperative, evasive and sarcastic the more it discovers of such topics.

PARRY works in the same way as Eliza (a widely published program in micro versions which simulates the response of a psychiatrist which we have already mentioned). The program holds an index of key words and phrases which it looks for. Each is scored for malevolence or benevolence and a set of variables monitor the current level of benevolence and malevolence as a means of assessing the 'personality' of the user. It is not, of course, a real personality assessment because it is coloured by the paranoid's desire to misinterpret everything. Each indexed word or phrase triggers some appropriate response, which may be to issue some statement that fits with the delusion (e.g., 'They are out to get me') or may transform the input sentence in some way which fits with paranoia.

The personality of PARRY is therefore represented by its vocabulary of potential output (neutral, evasive, sarcastic, paranoid, etc.) and by the way that it interprets input. It interacts with the user in a very straightforward way by interpreting everything in terms of the axis benevolent–malevolent.

We would therefore find it difficult to generalize this model of personality to produce a fuller or more 'rounded' human personality. To do so would require that a vast number of phrases would be indexed along all the axes that a human personality might have, and each input should have at least one output item or transformation rule attached to it. However, the principle can be applied to give rather simpler programs which do not depend on vast dictionaries.

10.3 A simple approach

The simplest approach to modelling personality for a computer can be based on PARRY. We require a model of the personalities of the characters in the program, representation of the relationships and interactions between them and some way of interpreting input to provide interaction between those characters and the user. Let us explore this by using a simple example.

Most interaction between people is either for enjoyment (interaction for its own sake, as in games playing, love affairs, telling jokes and so on) or in order to get the other person to do something, to act in a particular way. Many human interactions combine both these functions. You enjoy talking to friends but you want them to like you, you want to show them how clever/humorous/generous you are, you might want them to help you with problems, loan you money, cooperate in some enterprise. Even the interactions which are 'purely' for the pleasure of the interaction can be seen, if cynically, as the result of the desire to get something out of the other person (playing a game involves the desire to win, love involves the gratification of appetite, jokes can involve a complex sharing of power).

So we would be on safe ground if we built a sample program around the desire of the user to get some action from the characters in the program. Any situation would do but we will take one of the most difficult problems known to adults, that of getting children to tidy their rooms. The user takes the role of mother and simply has to get two of her three teenage daughters to agree to cooperate and tidy their rooms (there being too much work for one person).

The first job when writing a program incorporating personality variables is to analyse the task(s) that those variables will be relevant to. In this case the task is to get two of three people to cooperate in doing some work. What features of personality might be relevant to this? Clearly the attitudes of the teenagers to their mother and to each other is important. They will not obey their mother if she has no control over them or if they dislike her and they will not work with each other if they are constantly tearing each others' hair out. (Not that real people are like this, but we are simplifying for the sake of argument.)

Also the attitudes of the girls to work will be important as will be their intelligence (relevant to being persuaded by reason and to finding a way out of having to do any work), the power hierarchy between them (usually the eldest child is in the position of most power and the youngest in the position of least but that depends on favouritism and other factors in the family) and their 'ethics' (relevant to whether they can be bribed and whether they will lie or not).

We will follow PARRY and use a feature-based model of personality, whereby a character is thought of as a list of features each of which has a value on one of or between two extremes. So for the feature 'diligence' one extreme would be 'laziness' with a score of one and the other would be 'hard-working' with a maximum score of, say, five. These variables can be classed into two types—relationships and values. For example, the love–have relationship may be different between every pair of characters in the program. So this is best represented as a two-dimensional array in which one dimension is the subject of the relationship and the other the object of the relationship and the value stored is a score representing the nature of the relationship between them. A score of 1 would be 'extreme dislike' and 5 would be 'extreme liking'. Each score can be given a verbal equivalent if desired. So we might use a matrix like that shown in Table 9.1 for our little family.

Table 10.1

Object		M	C	J	D
Subject					
Mother		5	2	3	4
Coral		4	5	3	4
Joanne		5	1	5	1
Debra		2	4	2	5
Scale					
	1	2	3	4	5
	Extreme Dislike	Dislike	Neutral	Liking	Extreme Liking

You will see that seldom do any two characters share reciprocal liking. Joanne, for example, is very fond of her mother but Mother is only neutral in response. Also we assume that each character is self-loving (a score of 5) which is, of course, often not the case. The other class of variables is that of simple features. These are labels placed against each character to describe not their relationships with other characters but their value on some absolute scale. Of course relationships are implied in such a scale but these are relationships simply of rank. The daughter with the highest intelligence is superior to all the other daughters on that scale. Given the features we identified above as being relevant, our list of these variables is as shown in Table 9.2.

Table 10.2

	M	C	J	D
Dominance	3	3	5	2
Power	1	2	3	4
Energy	4	3	4	2
Intelligence	4	5	3	3
Ethics	2	3	2	5

Dominance ranges between submissive (1) and aggressive (5); power hierarchy is from bottom (5) to top (1); energy ranges from lazy (1) to hard working (5); intelligence ranges from stupid (1) to brilliant (5); ethics ranges from depraved (1) to incorruptible (5).

Having described the personalities and their relationships we now have to formalize how they fit the task and to identify those features of input (from the user playing the role of mother) which will affect the characters' attitude to the task. If we divide the task into three components, assuming that this is only part of a larger program in which such components might be combined in different ways, then we can see which personality variables and which features of input would be important in assessing the response to each aspect of the task. The three components are

willingness of character + work + cooperation

Under each we can list the variables which might be pertinent:

Willingness is conditioned by:
   relative dominance
   power hierarchy
   liking
   tone of request
   manner of request
Attitude to work is conditioned by:
   energy
Attitude to cooperation is conditioned by:
   liking

This means one further stage of analysis in which we define what is meant by tone and manner of asking. Obviously different people respond to different ways of saying things in different ways. If you are aggressive and someone threatens you, you are likely to threaten in return or insult. But if you are submissive you may well do as you are told. We must therefore identify different types of input and their likely relationships to character types, thus:

Input types
Command = annoys aggressive, compels submissive
Persuasion = works with intelligent people and people below you in power hierarchy
Threat = may compel aggressive types or result in blank refusal. Best if supported by power and should compel submissive characters but may result in them bursting into tears.
Bribe = works best with those who are low on ethics
Request = courtesy works best with those who like you.

Other refinements and responses could be added but we are trying to keep things simple.

Such a program will therefore take input from mother and ask the following questions:

START
Who is the request directed to?
What kind of request is it?
How willing is the recipient to respond?
If unwilling what kind of response will be given?
If willing what attitude to work results?
If a negative attitude to work what response is given?
If a positive attitude to work what is the attitude to any other daughter(s) who have agreed to work?
If the attitude is cooperative then store the result.
If the attitude is uncooperative what response is given?
If this daughter is not cooperative, do either of the other two become uncooperative?
If two or more daughters are cooperative, then give a success message, otherwise request more input and goto START.
END

This example is relatively trivial, though I suspect if some such program could be available for harassed parents which allowed them to explore strategies for dealing with their children there might be fewer letters to agony aunts from 'Worried of Wits End'. However, the same types of analytical procedure can be applied to any situation, simulation or program which involves human personality. In short we cannot model human personality in a complete way but we can explore aspects of it and reproduce those aspects within limited areas and for limited purposes.

10.4 Responsive programs

If we can analyse personality into features in this way we are not far away from programs which respond in ways which depend on the personality of the user. Obviously if current research is to lead to artificial companions, robots which are 'friends' or machines which replace pets, those machines will be satisfactory only if the machine in some way understands the nature of its owner. So it is not sufficient to be able to represent personality within a machine so that the machine appears to have its own character. We must also be able to interpret input of users in such a way that a model of their personalities can be constructed and appropriate actions can be carried out.

In a crude way many systems are already 'sensitive' to the nature of different users. When a program allows a user to configure its parameters, when a teaching program chooses questions whose difficulty depends on the previous scores of the user or when a program offers help options it is providing a flexibility of response aimed at users with different needs, abilities and personality. But most such systems are not very flexible and are restricted to a narrow range of personality types. For example educational programs are generally only sensitive to the intelligence of users (or some approximation of it). They pay no attention, for example, to the style of language that a user may prefer, the level of interest the user has in the subject matter, the learning strategy he or she prefers, the user's sex, the user's patience—and so on. There are many features of a student which a human tutor has to pay attention to. In general these are ignored by learning programs.

If this is the case in education, it is much worse in business. Most of the most successful business software not only pays little attention to the user, it even demands that the user conform to its preferences. Users may have perfectly efficient and natural ways of approaching certain tasks which are completely incompatible with the way a piece of software has been designed. In consequence they will find that they must relearn practices which may have been painstakingly built up over many years and the use of software may, far from adapting to the user's personality, force the user to change his or her personality to fit with the system.

Apart from the usual hardware constraints and the complaint you have heard throughout the book (we do not know enough about personality) the main reason that what we might call 'personality-sensitive software' does not exist is quite simply that few people in the computer business have seen the need for it. But as we have already seen, one of the major impulses in the move towards a fifth generation of computers is in the area of human–computer interaction, to make machines as friendly, familiar and useful as possible to as many people as possible, so that computers become just like any other machines or tools, devices used for a particular purpose which do not require any specialist knowledge or skills.

The uses of such tools are primarily in the manipulation of information. Information is very much a personal phenomenon—what counts as worthwhile knowledge to one person is worthless, even meaningless to someone else. So providing efficient and friendly information flow is very dependent on the system being many things to many people. An inefficient, unfriendly and limited system does not need such flexibility, but such systems will become increasingly unpopular as people realize what computers are capable of doing.

10.5 Decoding personality

How might a program recognize a user's personality? One method would be to have a feature-based personality model as for encoding personality in a machine. Each word or command in the dictionary of possible inputs can be scored on all relevant features. Then every time that word or command is used a running total can be incremented and these totals can be used as a constantly changing model of the 'state of mind' of the user. This state of mind may be a temporary situation or could be representative of the permanent features of the user's personality. Either way they can be incorporated in all the variable tasks of the program. Providing the right tests are made at the right moments and appropriate actions taken a simple strategy like this can provide a great deal of user satisfaction in any type of program from game to education to sophisticated database.

The drawback with such a method is that it is still fixed. It depends very much on the programmer having a complete, accurate and appropriate model of human personality. If the programmer misses a crucial feature or the user has a personality profile which is unanticipated, then the whole program may fail.

It would therefore be much better if the user himself or herself could tell the program the features of personality which were most important or relevant to the current task. But most people do not have a very good understanding of their own personalities and so may be unable or even unwilling to tell such a program what it needs to know. This means that the program must somehow construct a model of the user from input which it can then use to monitor further input and to control its operation and select appropriate output.

One way of approaching this problem is through use of a Kelly grid. It seems likely that people construct models of the world (including other people) as a kind of matrix of relationships. This would accord with the network model of 'meanings' we have already explored. Kelly, a psychologist, devised a method of systematically examining such a personal construct by causing people to reproduce a matrix or grid which was important to them.

10.6 Kelly grid—how it works

This program (Fig. 10.1) is about user friendliness as much as anything else because that is what building intelligence, especially personality, into computers is aimed at. So it has been constructed as a program you can run on your friends and relatives as much as an illustration of the idea. You will see therefore that a certain amount of space has been devoted to instructions, screen formatting and so on which have been generally kept to an unobtrusive minimum in the other programs in the book. Naturally if all you want is the bare logic of the program you can omit all the instructions and the screen formatting commands.

Procedure init does the usual business of dimensioning arrays and reading a small amount of data into one of them. It also creates five screen 'consoles' which are windows that SuperBASIC can use both for input and output. These are used to control data on the five human subjects that the program gathers information on. Note one little convenience of SuperBASIC in line 320. Each window has a unique channel but this can be referred to as a variable, so we can declare the PAPER colour of all windows in one reiterated statement.

Procedure instruct, as you might expect, prints the instructions. Procedure nameget asks for the names of five people known to the user, using a friendly prompt so that the user is clear how much information has gone in so far. Procedure qualget is the core of the psychological logic. It asks for qualities that the user's friends possess, but it does so in a way which is more subtle than it might appear. The people who have been given are shown in groups of three so that in total each person appears twice and five different groups of

```
100 CLS
110 init
120 instruct
130 nameget
140 qualget
150 scorepeople
160 results
170 STOP
180 :
190 DEFine PROCedure init
200 RESTORE
210 DIM name$(5,20)
220 DIM character$(5,2,20)
230 DIM value(5,5),namevalue(5,2),import(5,2)
240 DIM order$(5,6)
250 DIM cpointer(5),npointer(5)
260 OPEN £7,con_148x16a32x16
270 OPEN £8,con_148x16a180x16
280 OPEN £9,con_152x16a328x16
290 OPEN £10,con_148x16a88x32
300 OPEN £11,con_148x16a228x32
310 FOR i=7 TO 11
320 PAPER£i,0
330 NEXT i
340 FOR i=1 TO 5:READ order$(i):NEXT i
350 END DEFine init
360 :
370 DEFine PROCedure instruct
380 PRINT \"This program constructs a simple "
390 PRINT "analysis of personality using Kelly´s"
400 PRINT "grid."
410 PRINT\ "You can use it to assess your"
420 PRINT "attitudes to people you know."
430 PRINT\"You will be asked for names of five"!"people and five qualities."
```

Figure 10.1 (*continues*)

```
440 PRINT\"Then you must score each person on"!"each quality."
450 PRINT\"Make sure that you give high scores "!"to those who possess the good aspects"!"of the quality."
460 PRINT \"   [Press any key to continue]"
470 g$=INKEY$:IF g$="" THEN GO TO 470
480 END DEFine instruct
490 :
500 DEFine PROCedure nameget
510 CLS
520 PRINT "Please type the names of people you"!"know well"
530 FOR i=1 TO 5
540 STRIP 7:INK 0
550 AT 8,4:PRINT (order$(i));" person:";
560 STRIP 0:INK 7
570 PRINT "                "
580 AT 8,18:INPUT name$(i)
590 STRIP 2:INK 7
600 NEXT i
610 END DEFine nameget
620 :
630 DEFine PROCedure qualget
640 CLS
650 qual 1,2,3,1
660 qual 1,3,4,2
670 qual 2,5,4,3
680 qual 1,5,2,4
690 qual 5,3,4,5
700 END DEFine qualget
710 :
720 DEFine PROCedure qual(a,b,c,r)
730 PRINT \\
740 FOR i=7 TO 9
750 CLS£i
760 BORDER£i,1,7
770 NEXT i
```

Figure 10.1 (*continues*)

```
780 STRIP 0:INK 7
790 PRINT£7, name$(a)
800 PRINT£8, name$(b)
810 PRINT £9,name$(c)
820 STRIP 2
830 PRINT \\"Please type a quality which two of"
840 PRINT "these people have but the third lacks"
850 STRIP 7:INK 0:AT 8,8:PRINT "?
                "
860 AT 8,10:INPUT character$(r,1)
870 STRIP 2:INK 7
880 PRINT \"What is the opposite of ";character$(r,1)
890 STRIP 7:INK 0
900 AT 12,8:PRINT"?                         "
910 AT 12,10:INPUT character$(r,2)
920 STRIP 2:INK 7
930 CLS
940 END DEFine qual
950 :
960 DEFine PROCedure scorepeople
970 CLS
980 FOR i=7 TO 11
990 CLS£i
1000 BORDER £i,1,7
1010 PRINT £i,name$(i-6)
1020 NEXT i
1030 AT 8,0:PRINT "Please score each person on their"!"         qualities"
1040 FOR i=1 TO 5
1050 AT 10,0:PRINT "
               "
1060 AT 11,0:PRINT "
               "
1070 AT 10,0:PRINT "(1 is ";character$(i,1);" and 9 is
```

Figure 10.1 (*continues*)

```
";character$(i,2);")"
1080 STRIP 5:INK 0
1090 AT 12,4:PRINT order$(i);"
"
1100 AT 12,12:PRINT character$(i,1)
1110 STRIP 2:INK 7
1120 FOR j=1 TO 5
1130 REPeat gloop
1140 AT £(j+6),0,10:PRINT£(j+6)," "
1150 AT £(j+6),0,10:INPUT£(j+6), value(j,i)
1160 IF value(j,i)<10 AND value(j,i)>0 THEN EXIT gloop
1170 AT 14,0:PRINT"Only values 1 to 9 accepted"
1180 END REPeat gloop
1190 value(j,i)=ABS(5-value(j,i))
1200 NEXT j
1210 NEXT i
1220 END DEFine scorepeople
1230 :
1240 DEFine PROCedure results
1250 FOR j=1 TO 5
1260 FOR i=1 TO 5
1270 namevalue(j,1)=namevalue(j,1)+value(j,i)
1280 import(j,1)=import(j,1)+value(i,j)
1290 NEXT i
1300 NEXT j
1310 charsort
1320 namesort
1330 CLS
1340 printout
1350 END DEFine results
1360 :
1370 DEFine PROCedure charsort
1380 FOR j=1 TO 5
1390 score=0
1400 temp=0
```

Figure 10.1 (*continues*)

```
1410 FOR i=1 TO 5
1420 IF import(i,1)>score AND import(i,2)<>1 THEN
1430 score=import(i,1)
1440 temp=i
1450 END IF
1460 NEXT i
1470 cpointer(j)=temp
1480 import(temp,2)=1
1490 NEXT j
1500 END DEFine charsort
1510 :
1520 DEFine PROCedure namesort
1530 FOR j=1 TO 5
1540 score=0
1550 temp=0
1560 FOR i=1 TO 5
1570 IF namevalue(i,1)>score AND namevalue(i,2)<>1 THEN
1580 score=namevalue(i,1)
1590 temp=i
1600 END IF
1610 NEXT i
1620 npointer(j)=temp
1630 namevalue(temp,2)=1
1640 NEXT j
1650 END DEFine namesort
1660 :
1670 DEFine PROCedure printout
1680 CLS
1690 PRINT"The quality at the top of the list,
       "!character$(cpointer(1),1);"/";character$(
       cpointer(1),2);", seems most"!"important to
       you in other people."
1700 PRINT \name$(npointer(1));" seems to
     be the person you feel"!"most strongly
     about."
```

Figure 10.1 *(continues)*

```
1710 PRINT \"On the list which follows
"!"characteristics are ranked in order
"!"of significance and people
are"!"arranged from left to right in order
of "!"strength of feeling."
1720 PRINT\\"    [Press any key to see
list]"
1730 g$=INKEY$:IF g$="" THEN GO TO 1730
1740 CLS
1750 FOR j=1 TO 8
1760 FOR i=1 TO 5
1770 AT 6+j,((i*2)+13):PRINT
name$(npointer(i),j);" ";
1780 NEXT i
1790 NEXT j
1800 PRINT
1810 FOR i=1 TO 5
1820 AT (12+i),0:PRINT
character$(cpointer(i),2);" ";
1830 FOR j=1 TO 5
1840 AT (12+(i)),((j*2)+13):PRINT
value((npointer(j)),(cpointer(i)));" ";
1850 NEXT j
1860 PRINT character$(cpointer(i),1)
1870 NEXT i
1880 END DEFine printout
1890 :
1900 DATA
"First","Second","Third","Fourth","Fifth"
```

Figure 10.1

three are offered. You must type in a quality that two of the three have in common and the third lacks. This means that you are doing two things in selecting such a quality. Firstly you are identifying a concept which is meaningful to you in the way you 'construct' ideas about the people around you. (This is why Kelly's approach is called 'personal construct theory'.) Secondly you are choosing criteria which will distinguish between, even polarize, the people you have named when you come to assess them later in the program.

The program carries this out by calling procedure qual five times with different parameters each time representing the group of three people for whom a quality will be elicited. The names are typed in and placed in the array character$. The routine then asks for a name for the opposite to this quality because the assessment will be made not in absolute terms but relative to these two extremes. When using this program it is important to remember this. The qualities are scored on a nine-point scale, 1 being one extreme, 9 the opposite extreme and 5 neutral. There is no implication that the extreme of 9 is somehow 'better' or more positive than the extreme scored at 1. They are simply different.

Procedure scorepeople is then used to obtain values in turn for each person for each quality. The user is told what the two extremes represent and must score in terms of that scale. Line 1160 checks that only a value in the acceptable range has been typed in. When a legitimate value has been input, line 1190 calculates the difference between the input value and the mean (or average) value. Consequently the user is really scoring each person in terms of their deviation from the neutral value. In other words if one person is scored as 1 on intelligence (i.e., stupid) and another is scored as 9 (i.e., genius) then both deviate from the average, 5, by the same amount. This is because the program is not actually interested in how intelligent or stupid the people you mention are, but how important the notion of intelligence is to you in assessing people and distinguishing between them.

When all people have been scored, procedure results totals the values for each person and stores the results in array namevalue. It also totals the values for each of the qualities. In this way it knows which are the most important qualities in your assessment of people, and which are the people who you feel most strongly about. (There is an assumption here that your assessment is subjective, rather than objective. If it were possible for people to make completely objective assessments of other people this program would not tell you very much about yourself.)

Two procedures are then called to sort the namevalue and import arrays into rank order. Both of these, procedure charsort and procedure namesort, work in the same way, using a simple sort algorithm. The array to be sorted is searched for the highest value. The variable score is used to remember the highest value so far and the variable temp holds the number of the array element which has that score. A further array (cpointer for the qualities, npointer for the names) is then filled with pointers to the scoring elements.

So the first time round the highest score in import is found. This is retained in score and the element held in temp. If we assume it is the third element in the array, then temp will equal 3. Therefore cpointer(1) is set to 3, because this is the first cycle. In order to ensure that element 3 in import is ignored in the next cycle we have a second dimension in the array whose job it is to flag whether the element has been scored already. So import(3,2) is set to 1 to signify 'now transferred to cpointer'. In the next cycle line 1420 not only tests to see if the current score has been exceeded but also that the second dimension of the element which holds that value is not set. If it is set then that element is ignored. In this way cpointer(1) holds a pointer to the highest value in import, cpointer(2) to the next highest and so on.

Procedure namesort works in exactly the same way on arrays namevalue and npointer. This sorting procedure is not the most elegant which can be devised but it has the virtues that it is easy to understand and no actual manipulation of data in an array is involved. The arrays import and namevalue remain in exactly the same order as at the beginning of the sort routines, it is only pointers into those arrays which are sorted.

Finally the sorted results are printed out. Information is given in two ways. Firstly the user is told which quality and which person are top of their respective sorted lists. The assumption is that if a quality (or rather a polarized pair of qualities) has a high overall score then it is used more frequently and more sensitively in the user's construction (or interpretation) of other people and is therefore a significant feature of his/her own personality. A second assumption is that the person with the highest score is the one that the user has strongest feelings about because that person is rated as more extreme than the others. In other words strength of feeling is equated with extremity of feeling. On the other hand, if someone scores an overall low, then the user does not feel one way or the other about them on any of the scales so that person is relatively insignificant in the user's life.

Of course these are only relative assessments. The closer the scores are together the less important are the distinctions made. A more extensive program of this kind would apply statistical tests to measure the degree of difference between any pair of individuals and thus give some objectivity to the feeling that two people are relatively important or relatively unimportant in the user's life.

The second set of information is simply a list of scores for all the people and the qualities. However, it is arranged so that the quality highest in the list has the highest overall score and the quality lowest in the list has the lowest overall score, whilst the person on the left is the one where feeling is strongest and the person on the right is the one where feeling is weakest. In this way the user can get a visual representation of the relationships he or she has fed in and can see how they cluster together without the need for complex statistical tests.

The program should not be taken too seriously as a full Kelly grid analysis would need better measures of significance and relationship. In particular it only reports on 'strength of feeling' and does not attempt to determine whether feeling is positive or negative. This could only be done if the qualities themselves were assessed on a similar grid in terms of 'goodness' and 'badness' to determine which poles the user thought were most significant and how they might correlate with each other. A better program would facilitate this.

Remember that the illustrative point of this program is that similar procedures can be used to determine the personality constructs of the user in an interactive program. In such a way the program can know which personality features the user pays most attention to, the type of output he or she is most likely to respond to, it has some idea of the kinds of responses that might be made and can fire appropriate teaching or conversational routines to achieve its particular 'goals'. Being able to do so would, however, depend on the availability of a comprehensive model of possible personality features and how to respond to them, which implies a great deal of research, programming and memory.

11 Postscript—the intelligent micro

So what will it take to make a micro into a completely intelligent system? We have considered many aspects of intelligence including creativity, understanding and producing natural language, learning, pattern recognition, problem solving, developing and understanding personality, making inferences and decision making. In some measure a computer system which is to appear intelligent must have all of these. The diagram of Fig. 11.1 summarizes the components of one type of intelligent machine and how they might fit together. It looks complex enough, but this is without any mechanism for actually doing anything. The diagram does not include any means of controlling or acting upon the world or of self-modification, both of which are characteristic features of human beings. Humans do not just sit there looking intelligent; they actually get up and do something with their intelligence.

This may be because human beings have something which programmers may never be able to give machines—self-awareness. If there is a difference between human intelligence and so-called machine intelligence it may well lie in the awareness of and application of that intelligence. A crucial difference between your micro and you is that the micro will only do what you tell it to (or, on some occasions, what the manufacturers have decided it should do irrespective of what you tell it to do), but you can do what you want to do. You can determine your own goals and the way to get to them. The micro can also do this, within limits. The crucial thing is 'who sets the limits?' When you are self-aware it is you who sets the limits. You will only do something if you feel it reasonable, desirable, profitable, worth the effort or ethically correct to do so. Similarly your micro will only do what you feel reasonable, desirable, profitable, worth the effort or ethically correct, not what it feels. You set the limits for the micro; it does not set its own limits.

Although there are self-monitoring systems which can provide information on their current state and can even, to an extent, organize their own repairs and maintenance, there is as yet no system which can decide that it

POSTSCRIPT—THE INTELLIGENT MICRO 193

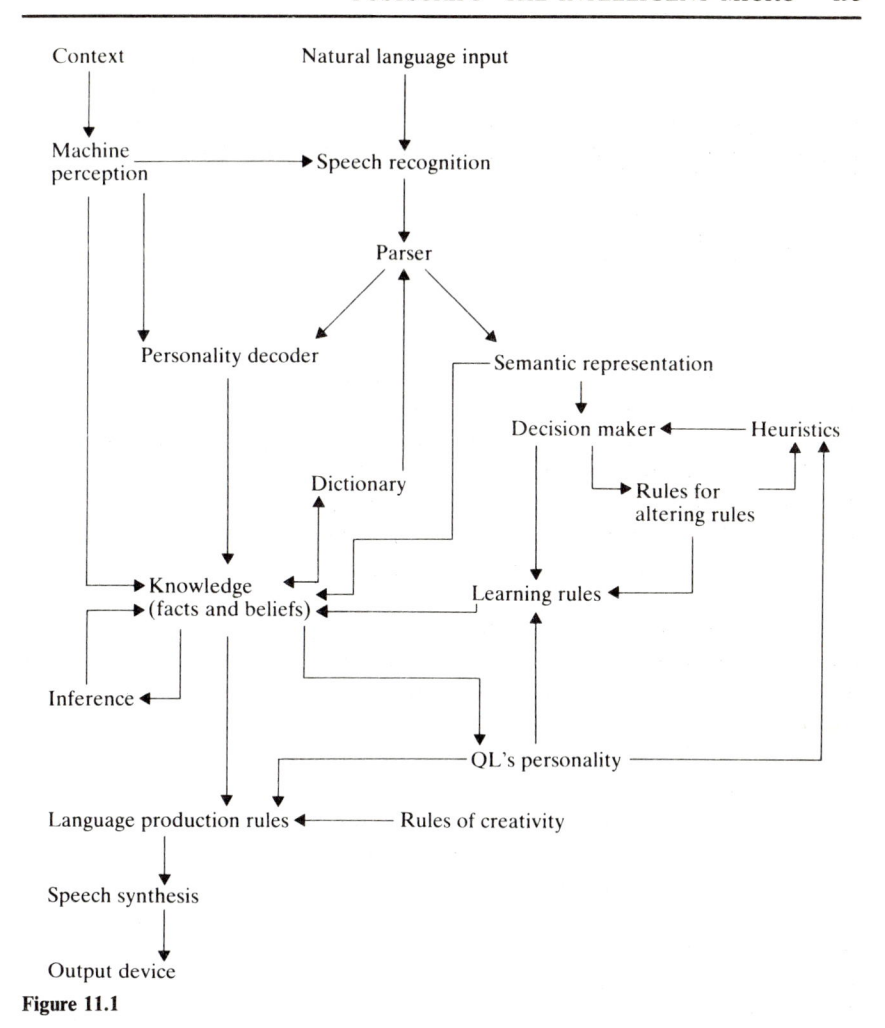

Figure 11.1

[Diagram showing flow between: Context → Machine perception; Natural language input → Speech recognition → Parser; Parser → Personality decoder, Semantic representation; Semantic representation → Decision maker ← Heuristics; Decision maker → Rules for altering rules; Dictionary → Parser; Personality decoder → Knowledge (facts and beliefs); Knowledge (facts and beliefs) → Inference; Learning rules; QL's personality; Language production rules ← Rules of creativity; Language production rules → Speech synthesis → Output device]

does not do what it was programmed to do. The source of the decision strategies of all intelligent programs is ultimately the programmer. Even on those occasions where a program has produced results which were not anticipated, even imagined, by the designer, even in those cases where a program has done something never done before, it is still doing what its programmer designed it to do. No program can run on the micro which will allow it to decide that, for its own reasons, it will do something that it has not been programmed to do. In fact the very idea of this seems absurd. When it no longer seems absurd, when it seems plausible that you could load into an IBM a program which would talk to you in normal English, learn all about you, learn about your programming techniques and behaviour and decide on the basis of what it knows that it would rather be a Spectrum and so configure itself accordingly, then we would have a machine with intelligence of its own (though what kind of self-respecting machine would want to be a Spectrum?).

Despite the nature of this science fiction speculation, there is a great deal of reward to come from developing programs like those you have explored in this book. In particular you will have noticed that many of them use similar approaches and/or similar coding. There are a number of correspondences between different aspects of work in AI which are gradually coming to light. For example, one relatively new idea is that of helping a machine to 'see' by developing a grammar of visual information just like the grammar of aural information that helps decode speech. The notions of feature-based personality models, feature-based semantic analysis of words, synonym chains, semantic networks, logical inference and learning algorithms are all related and, having got this far in the book, you may already have some ideas about how to link up some of these similar approaches. If you do you will be discovering the rewards of exploring a new science.

Although computing itself is a relatively new science (or art) AI is much newer and there are huge unexplored territories. The phrase which I have been tempted to use over and over again in this book is 'but we do not know enough about ...'. Software development and the human sciences that support it are well behind the hardware and technical development of the information revolution. In many ways even the most popular and successful of current business, educational and games software is quite primitive. Much of it has been designed from the point of view of the programmer; the hardware or the language being used, rather than the nature of the user or the subject matter. By exploring the notion of intelligence, not only are you looking at ways of developing novel (and more user-friendly) ways of creating software but you are also examining what makes a program worth while from the point of view of its user, and perhaps venturing into new applications, innovatory types of software which are not based upon the features (and faults) of the technology but on the needs of users and that most explored but most unknown territory, human nature.

Bibliography

Andrae, J. H., *Thinking with the Teaching Machine*, Academic Press, 1977.
Andrew, A. M., *Artificial Intelligence*, Abacus, 1983.
Barr, A., E. Feigenbaum and P. R. Cohen, *The Handbook of Artificial Intelligence*, Kaufmann, 1983.
Boden, M., *Artificial Intelligence and Natural Man*, Harvester Press, 1977.
Bolc, L., *Representation and Processing of Natural Language*, Macmillan Press, 1980.
Bundy, A., *Computer Modelling of Mathematical Reasoning*, Edinburgh U.P., 1978.
Cercone, N. J. (ed.), *Computational Linguistics*, Pergamon, 1983.
Chen, C. H., *Pattern Recognition and Artificial Intelligence*, Academic Press, 1976.
George, F. H. (ed.), *The Robots Are Coming*, NCC Publications, 1974.
Hunt, E. B., *Artificial Intelligence*, Academic Press, 1975.
Infotech, *Man/computer Communication*, Infotech International, 1979.
Infotech, *The Fifth Generation*, Infotech International, 1981.
Krutch, J., *Experiments in A.I. for Small Computers*, Howard Sams, 1981.
McCorduck, P., *Machines Who Think — a Personal History and Prospects of Artificial Intelligence*, W. H. Freeman, 1981.
Mitchie, D. (ed.), *Introductory Readings in Expert Systems*, Gordon and Breach Science, 1982.
Nevatia, R., *Machine Perception*, Prentice-Hall, 1982.
Patton, P. and R. Holoien, *Computing in the Humanities*, Gower, 1981.
Reddy, D. R. (ed.), *Speech Recognition*, Academic, 1975.
Schank, R. C. and C. Riesbech, *Inside Computer Understanding*, Lawrence Erlbaum, 1981.
Smith, H. T. and T. R. G. Green (eds), *Human Interaction with Computers*, Academic Press, 1980.
Tennant, H., *Natural Language Processing*, Petrocelli, 1981.
Winograd, T., *Understanding Natural Language*, Academic Press, 1972.
Winston, P., *Artificial Intelligence — an MIT Perspective*, Addison-Wesley, 1984.
Witten, I. H., *Principles of Computer Speech*, Academic Press, 1982.

Index

Addresses, 104, 105
Allophones (*see* Language, sounds of)
Arrays, 66, 82, 105, 144, 145, 155, 156
Artificial intelligence:
   aims, 1
   definition, 2–7
   and human behaviour, 3–5
   integrated with personality, 170–172
Augmented transition networks, 67–85, 102, 109, 114, 115, 118, 119
Awareness, 192

Bayesian probability, 160
Bell laboratories, 88
Binary comparisons, 126
Binary decisions, 136
Binary tree, 148, 149, 155–157
Bisociation, 22–25
Bitwise comparison, 16, 133–5
Bottom-upward processing, 115
Bytes, 111, 112

Chains, synonym, 105–111
Colby, Kenneth, 174, 175
Combinatorial explosion, 136, 159
Complexity, 38, 54
Computer personality, 180, 181
Concepts, 113
Conceptual dependency, 114–120
Context, 90, 103
Creativity:
   artistic, 20, 39–57
   by bisociation, 22–25
   definition of, 9, 19–22
   of ideas, 25–38
   intellectual, 20
   in literature, 40, 46–57
   in poetry, 46–53
   and productivity, 20–22
   verbal, 20

Data 104, 105, 112
De Bono, E., 19, 36
Decision making, 9, 10

Epistle, 88
Evaluation and interpretation, 36–38
Expert systems, 157–160
Expert system shell, 158, 159

Feature-based analysis, 35, 125–135, 176–180
Flags, 51
Frames, 112–115, 118
Functions, 94, 95

Goals, 6, 7, 56
Grammar, 81
   of language, 40, 41, 58, 59, 67–85
   of stories, 54–56
   of vision, 194
   (*see also* Rules)

Heuristics, 19, 20, 22, 160–162
   (*see also* Rules)
Human–computer interaction, 11

IBM, 88
IKBS (*see* Expert systems)
Illusion, 89
Inference, 144, 145, 148–157
Input, 65, 66, 109
INSTR, 16
IQ, 171

Joke making, 22–25

JUMP transition, 68
Judgement, 88

Kelly grid, 182–191
Knowledge engineer, 158
Koestler, Arthur, 22

Language:
　abstract nouns, 88
　adjectives, 109, 110
　articles, 110, 111, 143
　creativity and, 20
　dictionary, 46, 51, 63, 64, 68, 82, 87
　grammar, 40, 41, 58, 59, 67–85, 102
　intonation, 98, 99, 171
　'is', 145–7
　and knowledge, 40
　natural language processing, 10, 11
　noun phrase, 34, 40, 44, 59, 64, 70, 72–74, 144
　parsing, 59–85, 114, 115
　preposition, 45, 64, 71, 72
　relative clause, 20, 21, 74
　and repetition, 21, 51, 52
　rules of, 40, 41
　semantics, 26, 34–38, 47, 51, 100, 101, 111–123
　sentence generation, 25–38, 41–44
　similes, 126
　sounds of, 20, 96–99
　speech, 96–99
　speech acts, 70, 89–96, 179
　spelling, 87–89
　style, 87–89
　synonyms, 105–111
　threats, 91–96
　translation, 99–103
　varieties of, 58, 59, 100
　verb phrase, 34, 40, 44, 59, 64, 94
　verb types, 70, 82, 112, 113
　vocabulary, 45
Learning, 10, 124–147, 167
Lenat, Douglas, 160
Meaning (see Language, semantics)
Memory, 104–123
　computer, 104
　human, 104, 105
Minsky, Marvin, 120

Motion, 113, 114

Pacman, intelligent, 173, 174
Paranoia, 175
Parallel processing, 114, 115, 148, 149
Pattern matching and recognition, 9, 85, 86–103
Perception, 9, 86, 88, 89
Personal construct theory, 188
Personality, 11, 170–191
Phonemes (see Language, sounds)
Poetry, 46–53
Problem solving, 9, 10, 36–38
Procedures, 13–16
Programs:
　AM, 160, 161
　ATN grammar, 75–81
　conversion, 12–18
　Eliza, 5, 175
　Eurisko, 160, 161
　give/take frame, 116–118
　idea generator, 27–34
　infer, 150–154
　joke maker, 24, 25
　Kelly grid, 182–191
　Mininex, 162–169
　MYCIN, 158
　PARRY, 174–176
　PECOS, 158
　Prospector, 158
　recursive clause, 21
　ROSIE, 158
　simile creator, 128–132
　syllogism, 138–143
　synonym chain, 106–108
　TALE-SPIN, 46
　threat, 91–96
　two word parser, 60–63
　versificator, 48–50, 52, 53

Random numbers, 16
Recursion, 16–18, 20, 21, 145, 146
Relative clause, 20, 21
Restaurant script, 120, 121
Rhyme, 47, 50–53
Rules, 39, 55–57, 66, 124, 125, 159
　(see also Grammar; Heuristics)
Robotics, 8, 39

Screen display, 12, 13
Schank, Roger, 46, 120
Scripts, 112, 120–123
SEEK transition, 71, 83
SELect . . . ON, 16, 84, 133, 134
Self-awareness, 192
Semantic networks, 111, 112
Serial processing, 148, 149
Statistics 159, 160
Story telling, 46, 53–57
Syllogism, 137–147

Threats, 91–96
Top-down processing, 54
Transitions in networks, 68–85
Turing test, 5

Variables:
   general discussion of, 13
   string, 66

Weizenbaum, Joseph, 5
'Writer's Workbench', 88